The Fire on Our Hearth

A Devotional of Three Cranes Grove, ADF

Three Cranes Grove, ADF

Columbus, Ohio

Second Edition

www.threecranes.org
www.adf.org

www.lulu.com/garanus

This book belongs to:

_____

The Fire on Our Hearth **is a publication of Three Cranes Grove, ADF.**

Cover Art by Carmen Rose Howsmon
Cover design by James "Seamus" Dillard

Copyright 2010
Three Cranes Grove, ADF
[Compiled by Rev. Michael J Dangler]
[Individual authors retain their copyright]

Special thanks:
The 6th Night Grove, ADF, for inspiration to form this Grove, and teaching us to speak.
Sonoran Sunrise Grove, ADF, for further inspiration.
Ian Corrigan, for the work he has done that influenced our voice.
Jenni, Seamus, and the other Cranes who keep our liturgy organic.
Ceisiwr Serith, whose prayers have influenced, informed, and occasionally been stolen wholesale to make a liturgy work and to inform our voice.
(please pick up his books on prayer!)
Grove Members and others who have helped amass photos and drawings used in this book, particularly Jenni, MJD, Brian, Jim, Monika, Aeryn, and Erien
Carmen, Seamus, Lisa Lea and Shawneen for cover art and proofing, respectively.
Kirk, for proofreading and catching a *lot* of stuff we didn't!
All the other members of ADF who have written bits and pieces of liturgy we've used over the years.
Eris. You know, for not hurting us.

For more from Garanus Publishing, visit us on the Web at:

www.lulu.com/garanus

"Three Cranes Knotwork" cover art by Carmen Rose Howsmon

Table of Contents

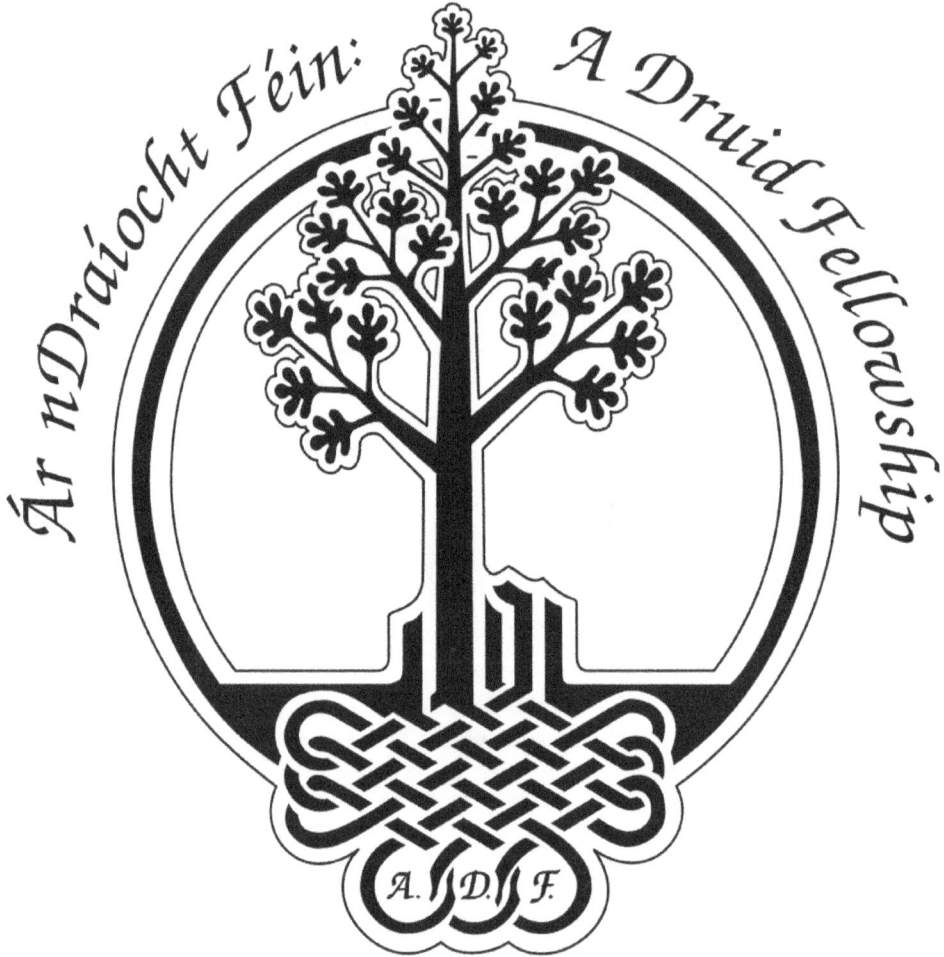

Introduction

"Let us pray with a good fire. . ."

-Rgveda I.26.8

Gracious greetings! You hold in your hands a small devotional booklet of rituals in the tradition of Three Cranes Grove, ADF. After eight years of doing ritual, working through the pain and the joys of public ritual, the Grove has certainly found a voice of its own, full of beautiful tradition, deep mysticism, and wonderful belly-laughs.

Inside this book, you will find solitary rituals for the High Days and bits and pieces from our liturgies, but these are of secondary importance to the joy of daily devotional work in the tradition of this Grove. Prayers for meals, rituals for self blessing, and meditations on the Grove's central mythology are all included here.

Three Cranes Grove, ADF, is named for the three cranes who were honored in Gaul for their connection to the God Esus. The mythology surrounding these cranes is lost, but their importance is still seen on inscriptions, and the Grove generally uses the crane, called *Garanus* (which is Gaulish for "with cranes," a nod to the fact that we are never without the cranes, though we use the name in the singular nominative often), as our Gatekeeper in rituals. This iconography has become vitally important to us, and the fact that its meaning has been lost has given us the opportunity to experience the meanings firsthand, and we hope that some of that meaning comes through in what we have written here.

There is mystery in this Grove, and this book can only offer a small glimpse, but we know that it will be a fulfilling glimpse. Come and join us in this tradition: sit around the fire with us in kinship, worship with us, and make sacrifice with us. All are welcome among the Cranes of Ár nDraíocht Féin.

This small book, then, is our attempt to collect much of our tradition, and to make it more widely available. As much as we love the Three Cranes tradition, we want to ensure that it is available to anyone who wants or needs these rituals or prayers.

So please, join us on this marvelous path, this winding trail that travels out from the world of the ordinary, through shady forests, beside the streams and rivers of our Mother Earth, always under the watchful eye of the Crane.

Bright blessings, and welcome to our Tradition!

-Rev. Michael J Dangler

The Flame of Our Druidry: Ritual in Practice

By Rev. Michael J Dangler

Nine Central Tenets of Druidic Ritual

In order to fully explain why we do the things we do, it's important for us to look at the entire vision of the cosmos: what are the assumptions we make about ritual, and how do they play into the eventual development of a "core order" or an outline of what we plan to do?

I've worked through a set of nine central tenets of Druidic ritual: things that every ritual assumes to be true, and that the cosmos we (re)create in every ritual can stand on its own. These are:

1. **Ghosti** – The reciprocal guest-host relationship.

2. **Rta** – There is an order to the world, and we are part of it.

3. **Hard Polytheism** – There are many individual Powers.

4. **Triple Cosmos** – A cosmos in three parts.

5. **Centered Ritual** – Our actions occur at the center of all.

6. **Fire** – We are a fire religion.

7. **Communication** – Not only can the Gods hear us, but they can respond.

8. **World-Affirming** – The physical is important and spiritually complete.

9. **Power & Responsibility** – What we do affects the cosmos.

Druidic ritual doesn't follow a set of beliefs: we are not an orthodox (right belief) religion, but a religion that values orthopraxy (right practice). As a result, the above list should not be taken as a set of "things you must believe in" so much as a set of ritual assumptions that make Druidic ritual structures work. These nine things get at the very mechanics of Druidry and how Druids participate in the Cosmos through ritual.

Ghosti

Druidic ritual is centered around our understanding of hospitality in the Indo-European world. It rests on the idea of **ghos-ti-*, which is a Proto-Indo-European word that exemplifies the idea of reciprocity and the guest-host relationship within an IE cosmos. What we do in ritual informs what we do in our mundane lives, as well, and we seek to exemplify this reciprocal ideal in all our relationships.

Hospitality has two sides: the good host and the gracious guest. A good host ensures that his guest is appropriately treated, and the gracious guest ensures the he does not overburden the host. Both guest and host are responsible for the maintenance of the relationship.

There is also the concept of "a gift for a gift," where we seek to give to the Kindreds so that we may open a relationship in which they may reciprocate (not in the *knowledge* that they will reciprocate, but in the *hope*). Our interactions with the Kindreds are based on the idea that "the same hands that reach out to give also reach out to receive."[1]

A "gift for a gift" is not a one-to-one exchange, though. It is not "I bought you a $15 meal yesterday: today, you have to buy me $15 worth of food." You would not participate in that relationship very long, and neither will the Kindreds. A ghosti relationship is more like having a friend with whom you have been to dinner so many times that neither one of you remembers whose turn it is to pick up the check. When the check arrives, you do not break out your tally sheets and calculators, seeking to determine who owes what and who paid for which meal last; instead, one person simply grabs the check and, should the other protest, the response is always, "Oh, I've got this one. You can get the next one." In these cases, the *relationship* is more valuable than the check could possibly be, and the understanding is that the second person values the relationship just as much and would have done the exact same thing if he'd been a hair faster.

Our relationship with the Kindreds is one of reciprocity, much like the friends at the dinner table, or the guest and the host. This is an ancient feeling, and can be seen even in the Rgveda, where Agni (the fire) is described as drawing the folk together as a guest draws together the family that hosts him at their hearth.

Implicit in this relationship is the idea that we *can* form relationships with the Kindreds: the gods and goddesses, the spirits of nature, and the ancestors are all interested and willing to form these sorts of bonds. Because of this, we seek to form these bonds in any way we can: through offerings of praise which come from our deepest hearts, offerings of work we have toiled over with our hands, and thinking on them and turning to them when times become difficult.

We know that the Kindreds find joy in these relationships and wish to enter into them just as we do. To that end, we work hard to enliven this reciprocity with word and deed.

---

[1] Ceisiwr Serith, *A Book of Pagan Prayer*

Rta

Rta is the order of all things. It comes from the Vedic word for the order of the cosmos: always fair, always impartial, and always just, unbending and correct.

Translations of the word vary: *rta* can be translated as "Truth" or "Cosmic Order" or "Cosmic Law," and each translation is correct in some cases and incorrect in others. The reason that we use *rta* instead of an English word is that there simply is no English word that can convey the meaning. There are cognates in other languages, such as *orlog* in Old Norse and *asha* in Indo-Iranian, or even the Proto-Indo-European reconstruction of **xartus* could also be used. For the purposes here, though, we will use the Vedic *rta*.

In the Rgveda, *rta* is said to cause the dawn to be born, the cycles of the day and night to continue, the seasons to move, and the earth and heaven to be held apart. It is divinely guarded and the divine is bound by it as well.

In our rituals, we are seeking to do things properly by the *rta*. When we choose to do things by the *rta*, we are choosing to take the right actions in the cosmos. In many cases, we might look on this as following in the footsteps of the gods, emulating them or following their directives or examples. One could look upon this as a sort of clear alignment with the Three Kindreds and with the forces they represent in the cosmos. While in the Vedas, this was marked by specific ritual actions at specific ritual times, with no possibility for deviation, we're much more fast and loose with our ritual structure.

Despite that, we still look to conform in some way to the order of the cosmos. The Core Order of Ritual is one way we conform: it provides the first level of structure and order on this chaotic world. The COoR is an example of cosmos (re)creation as a whole. From a point where the ritual begins; through to the description of the cosmos; past the sacralization and population of that cosmos; and even in the blessings poured forth upon us by the Kindreds, we are engaging in an emulation of the *rta* and following the example given to us by the Kindreds.

We also conform to the *rta* by offering sacrifice. Sacrifice is a vital part of our cosmology, and participation in the process of offering sacrifice is clearly something that aligns us with the Kindreds. Often, we are following a formula given to us by the Kindreds in some way (occasionally through a trickster figure, such as Prometheus, or through emulation of the way the gods make sacrifice).

A third (though not final) way we conform to the *rta* is through maintaining the Wheel of the Year. By keeping the times of the year sacred, and in celebrating key events such as the return of the sun, the waning of summer, and smaller events like the phases of the moon, we help to maintain and continue their progression. In doing this, we are keeping the *rta* on its course, becoming agents of the cosmic order ourselves and ensuring its persistence.

Hard Polytheism

Hard polytheism means that we stick very strongly to polytheistic worldviews, interacting with the various powers and spirits throughout the cosmos as if they are individual entities with their own complex thoughts, desires, and motivations. Rather than thinking that the deities and spirits are "archetypes," "reflections of a single all-pervading force," or "energy pools," we accept that the Powers are beings with their own agency and are entirely able to act on their own.

The Powers and Spirits we call on are also limited. Rather than thinking of them as omniscient (like Santa Claus) or omnipresent (like the Hindu Brahman), we think of them as limited in time and space, as well as in knowledge. This is clearly the way the ancients thought of their deities, and specific examples can be found in world mythologies: at the beginning of the Illiad, Poseidon is "away in Ethiopia," which allows the Greek fleet to sail; and in the Rgveda, Varuna, guardian of the *rta*, requires spies to ensure that the Cosmic Order is kept by humans.

This ritual assumption also helps what we do make sense rationally. If the gods and spirits are just buckets of energy, why make sacrifice to them? If they are all facets of a single greater "truth," why call on only one or two during the Key Offerings? If they have no agency or ability to think on their own, why ask them for anything? By making the assumption that the world is populated with individual beings, we are also free to make the assumption that these beings care for us, that they are willing to form relationships with us, and that we are dealing with divinity that is interested and invested in our well-being.

A vital note should be placed in this section: ADF and Druidry in general do not require that you have a specific belief about the gods and spirits. Rather, what we are discussing here is a set of ritual assumptions that make our rituals *work*. There are no rules about your belief: if you prefer Jung's archetypes or the henotheistic "god beyond the gods" outlook on divinity, that's great and wonderful. The issue comes down to practice: for our rituals to operate in the vision of the cosmos we have, hard polytheism is a central assumption.

Triple Cosmos

In Druidic ritual, the cosmos is divided in three parts. What these three parts are and who inhabits them is far less important than their actual number.

Often, we think about the world as Heavens, Midworld, and Underworld, but these are not the only options. They have become our most commonly used division, though, due primarily to the general western IE focus within ADF, and a lack of good resources for Celtic ritual.

In addition to a triple cosmos, we represent that triplicity with a triple center. As Druids, we most commonly represent our center with a fire (which supports and acts as a gate to the highest realm), a well (which springs from and acts as a gate to the lowest realm), and a tree, pillar, mountain, or other axis mundi (which serves as the center of the worlds and the path between them). More on the function of these symbols and the triple center will be said in the next section.

The three most common Indo-European divisions of the cosmos that can be used in ritual are these:

Underworld, Middleworld, Heavens

This is by far the most common cosmic picture we see in Indo-European cultures and religion, exemplified by the classical Greeks in particular. In this conception, the souls of the dead go to the Underworld, we stay in the Midrealm, and the Heavens are populated with the deities (and some heroic ancestors). This conception is particularly common among the Western Indo-Europeans, and the division (though not necessarily the same assignments of "who goes where") is common throughout not only the Mediterranian tribes of Greeks and Romans, but also throughout the Northern tribes, where the world is clearly divided into heavens and underworlds, with Miðgard in the center.

Terrestrial, Atmospheric, Celestial

This division is found in the Vedas in particular, and describes a very different sort of cosmos than the previous division mentioned. In this cosmos, there is no underworld, but the face of the earth (considered to be disc-shaped) is the "lowest" of the worlds: even the sun, after completing his journey, does not go "under" the terrestrial disc to reappear in the morning, but rather goes dark and returns along the same path. Some gods, such as fire gods, sacred drinks, and rivers reside in the Terrestrial realm. The Atmospheric realm is the realm of the clouds, and certain deities (storm gods, water gods, and some fire gods) are said to reside here. The Celestial realm, beyond the clouds and the vault of stars includes many other gods and spirits that embody celestial phenomena (such as the sun or cosmic order), and also the ancestors.

Land, Sea, Sky

Found particularly in Celtic lands, this division has also become a sort of "horizontal axis" that divides the Midworld or the terrestrial realm to match with the "vertical axis" of Underworld, Midworld, and Heavens, despite the fact that this triplicity is clearly a cosmic division (particularly to the continental Celts, who swore by these forces), and there are better attested forms of horizontal axes in nearly every IE religion: the five provinces of Ireland, the four dwarves of direction in Norse, the four winds in the Mediterranean religions, and the seven points or places in Vedism.

Centered Ritual

There is a Zuni legend that when the Water Skate was given magical powers by the Sun Father, he stretched his four legs out upon the waters.

His front right leg stretched first to the northeast, the place of the summer solstice sunrise; his front left leg stretched next to the northwest, the place of the summer solstice sunset; his back left leg then stretched to the southwest, the place of the winter solstice sunset; his back right leg then stretched to the southeast, the place of the winter solstice sunrise.

Where his heart then rested marked the "Center Place," the center of the land that is surrounded by the four seas and the heart of the Earth Mother. It is below this center, below the heart of the Water Skate which is the heart of the Earth Mother, that the village of Zuni was established.

At the center of the village, another center resides. This is on a permanent altar in the chief priest's house, where a heart-shaped rock (known as "the heart of the world") rests. Within this rock are arteries that reach toward the four solstice points.

These centers, it is easy to see, form a series of centers that are both atop each other in an obvious layering effect and also all the same in their overlay. None of these centers can exist without the others, and they seem to form around one another in ever tightening rings. Each center is itself, unique; each center is also all the other centers.

Eliade indicates that religion itself is an orienting force, one that gives us a focal point from which to make sense of the world. When we are in a profane state, one that is not sacred, we have no point of reference. It is only through the breakthrough of the sacred into the profane world, the hierophany, that orientation is possible. "The heirophany reveals an absolute fixed point, a center."

It is the finding of this fixed point, this center, which allows us to make sense of the world. If religion is indeed about finding ways to orient ourselves, to place ourselves in relative location to everything else, then we must find those centers, even if we must create them. The creation of those centers is similar to founding the cosmos.

Centers themselves are different from the rest of the world. They are places that allow this orientation, an orientation that the profane world cannot provide. Many of us are familiar with the *axis mundi*, or the axis of the world from Eliade. These cosmic pillars can only exist, according to Eliade, at the center of the universe, and all things extend about it. It supports the sky and finds its roots deep within the earth, and its presence is not an ordering force, but a break, a rip in the fabric of the profane world that allows the sacred to pour into and destroy the homogeneity of space.[2]

The destruction of the homogenous space is made possible by openings to other worlds, allowing travel and communication between them. In the case of the Zuni, there are four upper worlds and four underworlds that the *axis mundi* allows access to. Time also begins at the center, and mythical time exists at the outskirts of their cosmos.[3]

In Druidic cosmology, we find that the center of the world has three parts: Well, Fire, and Sacred Tree. Often, we think of the Tree as the *axis mundi*, but it is not

---

[2] For further reading on Eliade's theory of hierophany and centers, see *The Sacred & the Profane: The Nature of Religion* by Mircae Eliade. ISBN: 015679201X

[3] For the Water Skate myth and Zuni centers, see *New Directions in American Archeoastronomy*, edited by Anthony F. Aveni: Oxford, England: 1988. ISBN 0860545830. The article in question is "Directionality as a Conceptual Model for Zuni Expressive Behavior" by M. Jane Young.

the only center in ritual. Indeed, all the hallows are a center, and they combine to form the center. The center is not complete with only the tree, for while the tree grows high and is rooted deep, it cannot devour our sacrifices as the fire can, nor can it carry our voices to the depths of the earth as the well can.

Instead, the center must make use of all parts of the hallows: Well, Fire, and Tree. Beyond that, though, there is also the center of the earth, the heart of the Earth Mother, upon whose breast we build our Fire, root our Tree, and sink our Well. We establish the center above her heart, above the center of the earth.

The Grove itself has a center, the place in the middle of those Grove members gathered that the energies and the focus of the ritual are centered. Within each other, we find our own orientation, our own center: there is no stronger center, no larger axis, no more powerful hierophany than that of a Grove standing together, orienting themselves to one another, and finding their place in the centers others can offer.

Most important, though, is another center that must not only be found, but that the ritual cannot happen without: the center of ourselves. Each of us, within our own heart, must find the center of our beings, the inner center that allows us to stand in the center, to be our own *axis mundi*. From us, all things radiate, and within ourselves we can discover a rift between the sacred and the profane.

If we cannot find the center of ourselves, if the hierophany of our hearts cannot be seen, then others cannot find it within us. If the Grove cannot orient itself by combining these centers, then it cannot find the center of the earth, the heartbeat of the Earth Mother. If we cannot orient ourselves to that center, then we cannot orient our hallows, and the Well, Fire, and Tree will not stand at the center of the worlds.

Centers are unlike any other thing in ritual: they are where we establish them. Yes, they can appear naturally, and there are places that a center is more likely to appear than others, but to truly do the work of magic, we need to learn to establish them, to place them atop one another, to blend them and to maintain their distinctions. We must find them in ourselves, either through meditation or ritual, and we must learn to use the point of reference created by our own center to orient ourselves to the other centers around us.

As Joseph Campbell said, "The center is everywhere; the circumference is nowhere."

Fire

Of the three common gates in the Sacred Center, it is the Fire that is most important within Druid ritual and Druidic cosmology. It is clear that like the eastern Indo-European religions, our own has developed into a fire-cult.

This is a good thing, and sensible. Rituals can occur without wells, trees, portals, and shafts in the ground, but when we boil down the things that are vital to our religion, the one thing we cannot worship without is a representation of fire. Without fire, it is as if we are empty-handed when we invite the Spirits and Powers: we can offer them no way to warm themselves, we can offer nothing to them to satiate their hunger or slack their thirst, and we have no symbol to build a center around. Because of this, it is right to say a prayer to the fire any time one is kindled, and the kindling of a fire is a prayer in itself.

The fire also crosses the three divisions of the cosmos: kindled on the earth, the fire's flames leap into the atmosphere, and the pillar of smoke created supports the celestial realm. The fire is connected intimately with the celestial waters, often said to be born from them.

Our Grove often quotes a partial verse from the Rgveda: "Let us pray with a good fire." This phrase, from RV I.26.8, means many things to our Grove. It conjures images of not only a fire of piety within us, where we ignite that religious or spiritual fire, but also of the physical fire before us, to which we make offerings, giving a command to each: one that tells us how to behave in ritual, and one which tells the fire how to behave, as well. By "praying with a good fire," we recognize both the fire within and the fire without, the piety of both our belief and our actions: we do not come before our gods empty-handed.

The fire is intimately connected to the sacrifice. Agni, the Vedic fire god, not only devours the sacrifice, but he calls the gods forth to sit upon the sacrificial grass, and he transfers the sacrifice to the rest of the host of gods and goddesses, who (it is said) cannot be exhilarated without him.

It is also no coincidence that of all the Vedic gods, Agni is the most closely connected to humans and the guest-host relationship. The continuous presence of fire in the households of our Indo-European ancestors speaks to why this is. Across the IE spectrum, fire is spoken of as a friend to humankind, called a good guest, and connected with the ancestors (who kindled fire before we did). There is no sacred thing that is more often invited into the lives of those who follow an IE religion in general, and Druidry in particular.

In Zoroastrian ritual, the two basic cult objects are still fire and water, both of which are offered to in the daily *yasna* ritual. This ritual seeks to purify the fire, called the son of the Lord of Wisdom and placed in the south of the ritual precinct, which is the place of goodness and bounty.

In many ways, the fire is the counterpart of the priest, a sort of example that our own priests must follow. By bringing the deities to the place of sacrifice, by transmitting the offering, and by knowing the ways of the sacrifice, the fire is the perfect priest.

Fires also play an integral part in ordering the cosmos (as does the priest in IE religions), and this can particularly be seen in the use of fire to make a place habitable and to bring it into the dominion of humans. When he first arrived in Iceland, Thorolf Mostrarskegg marked out his land and then took fire around the borders in order to claim the land as his own. There is no clearer way than kindling a fire to inform all the Powers and Spirits that we are here, and we are prepared to receive the Kindreds as our guests.

And so we say:

At our center burns a living flame.

Communication

Druidic ritual is based not only on the idea that the Kindreds are receptive to our voices, accepting of our gifts, and interested in a relationship with us; but also that they will speak back to us, offer us gifts in return, and continue that relationship with reciprocity. Most importantly, the Kindreds understand us when we communicate with them, and have given us ways to understand them when they communicate with us.

Each Druidic ritual calls out to ask the Powers questions about our relationship. These communications take many forms and use many different sorts of symbol sets: ogham, runes, oracle cards, augury, and tarot cards are just a few of the methods that might be used in our rituals.

What is often most important is not necessarily the type of symbol that is used, but an intimate familiarity with the symbols and a knowledge of these symbols that is shared with the Powers. Communication goes two ways: both sides of the conversation must understand not only the symbols used to communicate, but also how those symbols are interpreted by the other side. This means that it is up to us to choose a form appropriate to the Powers and appropriate to ourselves, and to study that form in enough depth that when the symbol is drawn or the bird flies from south to north, we know and understand the message as it is intended to be understood.

There are several methods of taking an omen in ritual, and the questions vary from Grove to Grove and even Druid to Druid. Most will ask three questions. Three Cranes Grove, ADF, uses this set:

1. **Have our offerings been accepted?**
2. **What blessings do the Powers offer in return?**
3. **What further needs do the Powers have of us?**

We have asked these questions because they seem to get us the most detailed answers we can possibly seek. We hear from the Powers not only whether the ritual went well, but what blessings we might receive in the cup *and* any further instruction they may have to give. It is because of the breadth of response that is possible that our Grove has stuck with this format.

Other Groves ask a different series of questions, which changes the focus of the ritual a bit:

1. **What blessings do the Ancestors offer us?**
2. **What blessings do the Nature Spirits offer us?**
3. **What blessings do the Shining Ones offer us?**

The above three questions start with the assumption that the Powers have accepted the sacrifices given, and will be offering blessings in return for the gifts.

Hemlock Vales Protogrove, ADF, has settled on a hybrid, in which four questions are asked of the Kindreds:

1. **Have our offerings been accepted?**
2. **What blessings do the Ancestors offer us?**
3. **What blessings do the Nature Spirits offer us?**
4. **What blessings do the Shining Ones offer us?**

This, of course, solves the issues with the alternate three questions listed above, and also dispenses with the "three question" format that is so popular (sometimes, it's nice that things don't always come in three's).

For our Grove's Druid Moon rituals, we ask a different set of three questions, ones designed to learn different things about our Grove:

1. What is our Path?
2. On what should the Grove focus until the next Druid Moon?
3. On what should each individual focus until the next Druid Moon?

The idea with these questions was to look at how we have done in the past, consider where we are going as a Grove in the future, and think about how we, as individuals, can do work in our own lives for the next month.

Remember, too, that negative responses should always be considered a very real possibility. Resist the urge to turn a negative omen into a positive one, and always go with your first instinct. For a very frightening omen, you might think about flipping coins. Nothing says "honesty" like increasing the odds for a negative omen!

This communication aspect of Druidic ritual is very much dependent on the tenet of "hard polytheism" discussed above. The individual Powers have the ability to communicate with us and express their opinions and enhance their relationships with us through a set of symbols we share. Also, this is another "ritual assumption" that is integral to how our rituals work. However you see divination (as communication with your own subconscious mind, as a way to tap into the akashic records, or any other of a number of theories), in our rituals divination is between ourselves and the Powers is very much a real communication with real beings, where we ask a question and we receive an answer.

World-Affirming

Druidic ritual, as mentioned above, is firmly rooted in the Earth Mother. It is concerned not with inner worlds or reaching a higher spiritual plane, but with perfecting this world in order to bring the spiritual into the physical. Our concern with the physical even extends to those around us: Druidry is about our entire community, whether that community is made up of other humans, plants, animals, or Spirits.

In a Druidic world view, each person, plant, animal, and spirit is important to the world order: each plays a part in our own *rta* and the cosmic order as a whole. When we make sacrifice at our fire, we are bound together with those who have made sacrifice before us, and those who will make sacrifice after us. Ritual is a community-building event between humans and the Kindreds.

The most basic way to communicate with the Kindreds is through prayer, but so closely allied to the idea of prayer is the offering that we cannot begin to discuss one without the other. Offering, of course, is the act of bringing gifts to the Kindreds in order to establish a *ghosti relationship. Bringing things that we value to the Kindreds, and knowing that they value these things as well (for they see fit to respond to our offerings with blessings) indicates that the physical is sacred, as well as the spiritual.

18

Part of why we make offerings is because there is no real division for Neo-Pagans between the physical and the spiritual; indeed, the best sacrifices are somehow "touched" by human hands (thus the use of worked silver over raw ore, cultivated plants over picked wildflowers, poetry crafted from divine inspiration over pure awen, and the historic use of domesticated over wild animals). This realm is the realm we are concerned with: the Earth Mother, the sacred center, and the Kindreds are all best described as an integral part of this physical world. As a result, the idea that physical offerings might not be welcome is foreign to our conception as Neo-Pagans. Indeed, the act of offering is indistinguishable from the act of prayer: every prayer is an offering, and every offering is a prayer.

Importantly, too, the physical space of ritual, including things brought into the space from outside, can be considered sacred. Much as a sacrifice should be somehow "man-made" to show our care and the importance of the task of creating the gift, the tools we bring and the sacred center we create are all clearly a part of the cosmos during ritual. While in some traditions, there is a clear line between what is "sacred" and what is "profane" even outside of ritual context (see, for instance, the prohibition against ever using an athame to cut anything physical in Wicca, in or out of ritual space), a ritual implement in Druidic ritual is not something that must always be kept in the realm of the sacred. In some harvest rites, a sickle is used to cut down a sheaf of wheat: this is not a symbolic harvest, but a physical act that is a small example of the harvest that is now ended.

Our rituals are not built on symbols, but rather on exemplifications. Rather than signify something in the cosmos, we recognize that each part of the sacred center is made up of the "stuff" of the cosmos. Just as a swatch of cloth does not symbolize the cloth, but is a piece of the cloth itself, our ritual items and tools are not symbols, but actual samples of cosmic realities. In our rituals, the Tree is not a symbol of the World Tree, but its wood is a *part* of the cosmic World Tree. The waters of the Well are not symbolic of the cosmic waters, but they are drawn *from* the cosmic Waters. The Fire at the center of our ritual is not a symbol of the cosmic Fire, but rather a spark that *exemplifies* the cosmic Fire.

The easiest way to think about this is to compare how we talk about the sacred center in ritual as opposed to how we talk about a country's flag. When we speak of the well, we call it "eye and mouth of earth," "cauldron of inspiration," and ask it to "flow within us." We do not speak of what it "represents" or what it is "like;" rather, we speak of what it *is*. When we speak about a country's flag, we talk about what the colors *mean* and what the flag as a whole *stands for*.

Through praising things in the world, we also praise the spirits who inhabit this world and the beings that created it.

Power and Responsibility

As we stand at the center of the worlds, we have the ability to affect all things and all times. Here we stand at the foot of the World Tree, the Fire burning brightly and raising our words to the heavens, while the Well resounds with our voices and sinks them down to the world below. Everything in ritual is a piece of the cosmos, active and present in a way that we can affect it.

When we call out to the Kindreds, they come to our fire. They listen to our words, and they receive our sacrifices. As part of the worship bargain, they offer blessings to us in return. The Earth Mother, who we love and honor, is given sacrifice so that she will uphold us and keep us throughout the rite, as she does each day of our lives. We call upon old bargains and long relationships with various beings, including the Gatekeeper, who we trust to guide and ward us as we walk these Elder Ways. We affect the cosmos in mighty ways each time we enter ritual space.

It is important to note, however, that as we do these things, we also affect ourselves and our communities. We are a part of the cosmos, and a part of the world.

Because all things that we do affect the cosmos, it is important that we remember that we must be good hosts and good guests. Our courage to work magic in ritual must be tempered by the integrity to work the right magics.

No matter what, standing in ritual is not about the individual doing the work, but about the relationships formed and strengthened by the work that is done. ADF teaches of Nine Pagan Virtues, and as we work ritual we must remain aware of them, for each affects the cosmos as well as the self.

The Nine Pagan Virtues are wisdom, piety, vision, courage, integrity, perseverance, hospitality, moderation, and fertility.

Wisdom is the intersection of knowing what is right and making the decision to do that right thing. By understanding the patterns of the cosmos and choosing an action that is right with it, we have made proper use of the power that ritual provides for us.

Piety is the intersection of belief and right action, with an emphasis on *right action*. Piety itself is the undertaking of an action that is right in the cosmos. It is observance and work in reciprocity with the beings who inhabit the worlds.

Vision is the ability to see what is right in the cosmos, understanding the connections between things, and understanding where the connections lead.

Courage is "doing what needs to be done," especially in the face of fear. The thing that needs to be done is not always easy, nor is it always clear; however, vision and wisdom will help one decide on the correct course to take.

Integrity is being "whole." This means internally (eating right, exercising, and staying healthy), communally (participating in the world in a way that benefits others), and cosmically (maintaining agreements and relationships, keeping our word, and sacrificing). Only by being healthy can we do ritual; only by seeking to benefit others in ritual can we work ritual with meaning; and only through the act of sacrifice and keeping our word can we interact wholly with the Kindreds.

Perseverance is meeting adversity and overcoming it. It is the manifestation of motivation, the end result of having the desire to do something right in the cosmos.

Hospitality, as we have discussed, is a central virtue in ritual: it is the *ghosti-relationship*, where we enter a joyful partnership with the Kindreds and offer them gift for gift, sacrifice for blessing, and they enter this relationship with equal joy.

Moderation is the knowledge of limits and necessity, the striking of balance in our lives. It is joy in the ordinary and seeking the spiritual.

Fertility is not just creative ideas, but creativity that is maintained. It does not exist in unfinished projects, but in the end result of the projects.

These Nine Pagan Virtues apply directly to what we do in ritual. They are vital to keep in our hearts and to be mindful of in our actions. It is not about us, but about things being right in the cosmos. It is about the *rta*. Let us do what is right with the power we have in ritual, for only then can we do what is right at all.

Prayers

These are simple prayers, said over a meal, on waking, in the shower, or any other time. Some are said often, and some rarely. Some are spoken before casting a ballot in a national election, while others are said before a business meeting.

As a Grove, our Paganism is a living Paganism, one that is tied to the cycles of our lives, and we are spiritual beings in the Grove and in the grocery store. As such, our prayers reflect very normal, daily sort of ritual.

Cosmos Prayers

One of the functions of ritual is to re-describe the cosmos. We do this at numerous points in ritual, but these prayers are particularly good for re-centering yourself or the folk at any time.

The prayer we most often use is this one, by Ceisiwr Serith, and you will find it in nearly every ritual we do. We also begin most of our meetings with this prayer:

Blessings, Honor, and Worship to the Holy Ones
By Ceisiwr Serith

The waters support and surround us
The land extends about us
The sky stretches out above us.
At our center burns a living flame.
May all the Kindred bless us.
May our worship be true.
May our actions be just.
May our love be pure.
Blessings, and honor, and worship to the Holy Ones.

The Grove has also come to use this prayer at the start of all our rituals now, as it describes the cosmos prior to the ritual, and works to help center the Grove.

Opening Prayer

By Rev. Michael J Dangler
(heavy influence by Ceisiwr Serith)

The spirits of the sky are above us.
The spirits of the land are around us.
The spirits of the waters flow below us.
Surrounded by all the numinous beings of earth and sky and water,
Our hearts tied together as one,
Let us pray with a good fire.

Meeting Prayers

The Grove has a standing tradition now of beginning every meeting with a prayer. For this, we most often use Cei's prayer, "Blessings, Honor, and Worship to the Holy Ones."

In addition to the prayer above, the Grove has spoken prayers to Mercury before meetings, to aid in negotiation and eloquence.

Mercurial Business Meeting Prayer

By Rev. Michael J Dangler
(inspired by Ceisiwr Serith)

As we meet today, bring us eloquence, Mercury.
Ease the way, remove all obstacles.
Open the way for smooth outcomes
Open the way for a productive meeting

Mealtime Prayers

Many of us speak prayers at mealtime. Some are quick and some are elaborate, but all of them recognize the sacrality of life.

Summerland Meal Prayer

By Rev. Michael J Dangler

O Earth Mother, ever bountiful and always full of life, we thank you.
To our Ancestors, who learned and taught us how to reap the bounty of the land, we thank you.
To the Spirits of Nature, green-kin and animal-kin who gave their lives that we might live ourselves, we thank you.
To the Shining Ones, bestowers of bounty and providers of blessings, we thank you.

Short Meal Blessing

By Rev. Michael J Dangler

Thank you, Spirits of Nature,
You who give of yourselves
That we may survive.

Thanksgiving Meal Blessing

By Rev. Michael J Dangler

Within each of us burns a bright fire:
A fire of fellowship and community.
As we come together today
Guest and host, family and friend,
Let each of these fires be magnified by the others
And bring us together in warmth and love.

Meal Prayer, Trillium 2008

By Rev. Michael J Dangler

We honor the Spirits of Nature
Who have given that we may live,
Our Ancestors who taught us to sacrifice,
And the Shining Ones ever in our hearts.
With praise to the Kindreds,
Let our meal be blessed.

At the evening meal (or whatever is the main meal of the day), it is appropriate to honor Vesta, the living flame, who is associated with the cook fire and the Penates. If you live alone and have irregular, quick meals, make a point of offering to Vesta a bit of whatever it is you're eating whenever you do sit down for a meal. Ideally, a place should be set for Vesta at the table with a serving of all that which the family is eating, then after dinner, but before dessert, the contents of the plate be cast into the fire on the hearth. As the offering is made, a short prayer to Vesta is made:

Daily Meal Prayer

By Rev. Jenni Hunt

Salve, Vesta Mater!
Greetings, Mother Vesta!
Accipe hoc sacrificium factum meo artificio de tua auxilia beata.
Accept this offering, made by my own handiwork with your blessed help.
Te precor humiliter uti sis volens propitia foco meo, domique familiaeque meae.
I humbly beseech you to bless my hearth, and the home of my family.
Macte hoc sacrificio.
Be thou increased by this which I give to you.
(Throw the offering to the hearth (or place it in the offering bowl, as the case may be).
Dea propitia sit!
May the Goddess be favorable!

Meal Blessing

By Rev. Michael J Dangler and Maggie Collins

We come together at this table to celebrate one another and each day.
Kindreds, we ask that you bless us with your company.
Thank you for the food before us, to nourish and sustain the body,
and thank you, too, for those beside us, who nourish and sustain the soul,
for you have given to us today, that we may give to you tomorrow.

The next prayer was written as a Discoridan Meal Prayer, meant to be spoken with tongue firmly in cheek (but take it out before you start eating: you might bite it!):

Discordian Meal Blessing

By Rev. Michael J Dangler

Eris Good and Strong and Bright,
Make this food safe tonight.
Anthrax, chicken pox and hugs,
Please keep at bay such thugs.

Kitty claws and dragon teeth
Do not contaminate my beef.[4]
My veggies and salads green
Are not replaced with dolphin spleen.

Eris, O Mother Discordia and Poof
Take this as prayer, not spoof.
Through your guidance and strife
May we see our lessons in life!

Several of our members have written family prayers that they say at each meal. Here are prayers and an explanation from Shawneen and his family:

"So that they don't become stale and without true meaning, my family has taken up the custom of writing a new meal time prayer for each season. My family members rotate each season so that the prayer is renewed at least 4 times per year. The following are examples from each season that have been recorded in our prayer book (we keep a copy of all prayers the family has written)"

Winter Solstice 2006

In this time of Rest and Renewal, let us Re-think, Re-link, Re-create and Re-store.
Let us Re-member that We are the living waters!
   that We are the Holy Crystals!
   that We are the New Kingdom!
   that We are the Stars that Sing!
Let us Re-joice and make a joyous noise!
Bíodh sé amhlaidh!

---

[4] Vegetarians may change this to:

Kitty claws and dragon sneeze
Do not contaminate my cheese.

Spring Equinox 2006

With spring comes new growth, new plans and new ideas.
Bless this meal and help us to walk in balance upon Mother Earth!
Bíodh sé amhlaidh!

Summer Solstice 2005

Let us walk the path of peace and harmony together!
Each of us is responsible for the world we live in!
 Bíodh sé amhlaidh!

Autumnal Equinox 2007

In this time of harvest,
Let us be truly grateful for our many, many blessings.
Let us remember to share our ingathered fruits with those less fortunate.
Help us to be mindful that wealth fairly shared is wealth multiplied.
Bíodh sé amhlaidh!

Morning Prayers

Starting your day with a prayer can change your entire outlook on the day. Here are some example prayers that Grove members use.

Integrity Prayer
By Rev. Michael J Dangler

Today, Integrity
To be who I am
To know what I want
To speak with my own truth
To show the world myself.

Prayer to Dawn
By Rev. Michael J Dangler

Early this morning,
The birds began to sing:
Cries and crows,
Joyful and bright.
They sang and called
Praising the beauty of dawn
And through their voices
Gave her birth.

Warrior's Morning Prayer
By Seamus

Hail the Shinning Ones
Thank you for your blessings
May you continue to watch over me
May I walk in Blessings!

Hail the Ancestors
Thank you for your sacrifice
May you continue to guide me
May I walk in honor!

Hail the Land Spirits
Thank you for your lessons
May you continue to teach me
May I walk in balance!

Today is a good day and I stand as a warrior
Ready for the call of duty
I walk in blessings, honor and balance
If today is my last day then may I die as I walk...
In blessings, honor and balance

This prayer, to Epona, calls on the horse goddess' aspects of protection and nurturing. The word at the end, "Esti," is Gaulish for "it is," an equivalent phrase to the Judeo-Christian "Amen."

Morning Prayer to Epona
By Rev. Michael J Dangler

Epona
I light your candle
Make offerings to you
And stand before you humbly.

Protect me this day;
No matter how fast I travel,
No matter the distances covered,
No matter who I encounter:
Guide me, protect me, nurture me.
Esti.

The following prayer is designed to be said in the shower each morning (it can be changed to an evening devotional if you change two key words: "morning" becomes "evening," and "start" becomes "end").

Shower Devotional

By Rev. Michael J Dangler

Good morning, waters.
I feel you as you flow over me
Washing away the dirt
Washing away the cares
Washing away stiffness.
You wash away so many things
So I may start my day renewed.

Another sort of prayer might be for the dawn. This prayer was written to be said at each dawn, and is addressed to the Vedic goddess Usas. It is beautifully bookended by the prayer to Ratri in the next section, Evening Prayers.

Dawn Devotional Prayer

By Rev. Michael J Dangler

A maiden dancing, dancing
on the rim of the world
Resplendent, Radiant
I blush to see you rise from your bath
the colors of the sky drip from your bosom
as you open the ways for the sun
Greetings, Usas, who opens the gates of heaven.

For Dawn

By Seamus

The silent sycamores stand at attention along the winding creek,
holding vigil through the night.
The cold of the morning rides in on the winter wind
as the snow reflects the coming of the light.
Another lipstick sunrise is smeared across the sky
as red gives way to blue.
Father Sun kisses Mother Earth and whispers,
"I love you."

Evening Prayers

Evening prayers can help drive away the stress of the day, calm you, and prepare you for bed. These prayers are well suited to being said at sunset or just before retiring.

Sunset Devotional Prayer

By Rev. Michael J Dangler

Ratri, daughter of heaven
weaving the web of sacrifice
and conducting my prayers with bright rays.
As Usas comes each morning, so do you at night
Cloaked in stars, brightly shining
Maintaining the order of our lives.
Allow me to sleep, my head in your lap
As you sit upon the sacrificial grass.

Sunset Devotional
By Irisa

Hesperides,
Daughters of the Night
Guardians of the tree of golden apples.

may your sweet song
bring the golden glow
of the sun's radiance
to rest for this day.

may your wisdom and spirit
guard this hearth and home.

Hesperides,
Daughters of the night
comfort all who rest
within these walls and on this land.

This prayer is addressed to Epona, and can be said at the end of every day, working in concert with the morning prayer to Epona in the previous section (it in fact mirrors the other prayer entirely, with a slight wording change, but since both prayers are in common use, both are provided).

Evening Prayer to Epona
By Rev. Michael J Dangler

Epona, I light your candle
and stand before you humbly

You have protected me today
No matter how fast I traveled
No matter the distances covered
No matter who I encountered.

For guiding, protecting, and nurturing me
I thank you.
Esti.

Prayer to Baldr at Sunset

By Seamus

As the light fades to the west and the sky is streaked orange and red
As the hills fade to their golden canopy.
In the twilight we see the long decent of Baldr's funeral pyre.
As Hringhorni burns goodbye.
Even now as Sleipnir thunders over the bridge of Gjöll.
Hermóðr the brave rides to the halls of Hel
All but one mourns the lost.
Hail Baldr!

Prayers for Protection

Often, we feel like we are in danger, like no one is watching out for us. At those times, it does us well to have a prayer handy to overcome our fears.

In this first prayer, a mantra meant to be spoken over and over again, the petitioner asks Indra, the Vedic storm god, not to strike him with his lightning bolt (implying that Indra's strike be true and release the waters upon the earth).

Prayer for Frightening Storms

By Rev. Michael J Dangler

Indra, protect me. Strike me not.

Prayer to Skaði for Safety in Snow Storms

By Rev. Michael J Dangler

The cold winds bluster about me
The clouds are so heavy and gray
The spring snows fall all around me
Making the pathways dangerous.

Skaði, you travel the mountains
Through the ice and the snow and winds.
Guide me now as I travel this path
Guide me as I find my way home.

Prayer for Travelers

By Anna Banana

O Teutates,
My kin travel far from me.
When the time is proper,
Bring them home safely.
Let the tribe reunite.

Healing Prayers

As the Grove has become more involved with healing over the years, and as the Order of the Crane is now developed, prayers for healing have become more and more important to our work.

This prayer was written for our Grove Priest's father, but when originally published was published with "blanks" instead of specific names so that others could also use the prayer. It calls on the "shining" nature of the deities to engulf the person in need of healing, to let the blessings of the deities roll over and brighten the person.

It is, in many ways, a prayer that asks that the shining light of the deities warm and comfort the person who is in need of healing.

Healing Prayer to the Shining Ones

Rev. Michael J Dangler

Shining Ones,
Your light stretches far,
Bright and holy,
Showering blessings like waters from heaven.

Spread your arms wide,
Embrace _____ warmly,
Let your light shine forth,
Blessings out and down,
Rolling over [him/her]
Brightening [his/her] body and soul.

Shine upon ____.
Heal [him/her].
Make [him/her] bright with your touch.
Esti.

Healing Prayer to Eir
By Rev. Michael J Dangler

There is a maid at Mengold's knee,
Who knows the ways of healing.
Upon the healing mountain she sits
And draws the cool waters from below
These waters she brings for those who come
A gift within their open hand
And pours them out upon the pious
To make them whole and free from harm.

Civic Prayers

A civic prayer is any prayer that looks out for those around us, that deals in large, community-oriented issues. These prayers support the social order, and can be said any time we are doing our civic duties.

One time might be when we go to the polls. Here is a simple prayer that can be said while in the booth, before voting.

Prayer for Voting
By Rev. Michael J Dangler
(adapted from a prayer by Ceisiwr Serith)

Gods and Goddesses of our people:
As we go to the polls today
To choose leaders of integrity and courage
May our choices be guided by wisdom and vision.

Often, too, we pray for the community at large, or for those who need more help than we can provide. Here is a prayer for the hungry, said before the canned goods we collect at our rituals are dropped off at the local foodbank.

Prayer for the Hungry
By Rev. Michael J Dangler

There are those who are hungry tonight
Who were hungry yesterday, and the day before.
Spirits of this land, help us to provide for them,
And tell the Spirits of other lands how to do the same.
Let their hunger be in the past one day soon:
Only a distant memory of hard times.

There are those who live their lives in service, from police to firefighters to soldiers to EMT's. This prayer is for them.

Prayer for Those who Serve

By Rev. Michael J Dangler

When order is broken, you are there.
When hungry fury swirls, you are calm.
When children see warfare, you shield them.
When our bodies break down, you mend them.

Blessings of the Kindreds upon you,
You who are always there when we need you,
You who protect and serve us,
Even when we forget you are there.

Prayer for Peace

By Carmen

I am capable, every day, of giving myself something that I need, and every day I am also capable, of giving someone else, something they need.

Every thought, every action, every breath feeds ourselves as well as our neighbors.

Kindred, remind me of the reverence of life, that death and change is as part of life is our birth, as well as the birth of our ideas.

Kindred, help me to feel and find this peaceful connection at all times, but especially when I feel most alone. Help me to help others feel and find a happy stillness in the hurriedness of this busy world.

Prayer for Mothers

By Rev. Michael J Dangler

Let the light of a mother's love
never diminish in a child's heart.
Let the light of a mother's love
never diminish in a child's eyes.
Let the light of a mother's love
never diminish in a child's memory.
Let nothing come between mother and child,
and let the child always know the mother.

Shawneen, who has often acted as seer for our rites, drew an omen for the inauguration, as well. Though not a prayer, it fits well here. He presents it as follows:

Oghams for a new President

By Shawneen
Jan. 20th, 2009 | 03:57 pm

After watching the inauguration of President Barak Obama, I was moved to do an ogham reading for the occasion of his new presidency. Here are the results:

- Influences from the past: ⊣
  - *Ngetal*/the broom "we have to heal the past to move forward into this new time"

- Influences of the present moment: ≣
  - *Eadha*/the aspen "The message on the wind...the man's words speak for themselves"

- Influences from the days to come: ⊒
  - *Saille*/the willow "Intuition and lunar watery female viewpoints will be key"

- Overall tone for the administration: ⊫
  - *Quert*/the apple "the choice has been made, love will be key"

"By healing the wounds of the last administration, moving forward with his vision, using love and intuition and real family values the administration will be a success....these are good omens"

Anna Banana created this prayer for the 2008 inauguration of President Obama. She wrote: "Sometimes I pray for the protection of our president. I have no set script, but today during the inauguration I primarily prayed that no ignorance or hatred would bring him harm."

Protection for Obama

By Anna Banana

Kindred, please protect Obama.
Shield him with truth and with hope,
that no amount of hatred bring him harm.
Let ignorance cower.
Let our President fulfill the oath he has sworn to this nation.

In 2004, Ohio passed a ban on same-sex marriages. Since then, the clergy and members of Three Cranes Grove, ADF, have become more and more deeply involved in movements that seek equality and justice for all people. While the Grove does not endorse political candidates or specific issues, we do endorse the fundamental human right of every person to love as they see fit. These prayers are a result of our interfaith work with the marriage equality movement, the gay pride movement, and our general acknowledgement that all human beings are a part of our community deserve the same respect any others are afforded.

Prayer for Equality of Love

By Rev. Michael J Dangler

We are all Children of the Earth,
Equally drawn from her bosom
And formed by divine hands.
Each of us is animated by the same breath
And given the same capacity for love.

As we march upon the Earth seeking justice,
Let the Earth Mother support us
And the divine show us the heights we may reach.
Let our voices arise as smoke from a holy fire
And our words resound in the depths of the world.
Let all who love, love equally.

Prayer for Justice

By Rev. Michael J Dangler

Within each of us, we find a just balance:
A well of caring and love within our hearts;
A fire of knowledge burning brightly in our heads.
With these two working in concert,
We know right from wrong
And can fight for justice
And recognize inequality where it stands.
As we seek this well and this fire within ourselves,
Let us be ever mindful of the balance they bring,
And joyous at the light their synthesis brings
To shine out and cleanse the darkness of hate and fear.
Let us be filled with this light,
Let the work of our hands spread it,
And let the joy in our hearts compound it.
So be it.

Gay Pride Parade Prayer, 2008

By Rev. Michael J Dangler

"I am Rev. Michael J Dangler, of Three Cranes Grove, ADF, a local Druid fellowship. We have always felt it was important to celebrate Pride, for we are all Children of the Earth Mother. Whether we believe were formed from clay and given life by the breath of a deity; made up of the elements of the periodic table; or born directly from the Mother herself, we all share our one Earth Mother. As we prepare to depart, we will ask for blessings from our Earth Mother this day. Thank you for coming to this service, and thank the organizers for holding it. It is our tradition, though you need not follow it, to kneel and touch the ground as we call out to the Earth."

Earth Mother, your children call out to you.
You uphold us as we move through life, with each step we take.
Let every step we take upon you today in pride and unity
Be a step toward justice, understanding, and love.

Let us follow the footsteps of our Ancestors
Who blazed trails long before us and fought for what was right.
Let us hear the blessings of the Nature Spirits
Who play among the trees and upon the wind.
And let us go forth with the strength of the Shining Ones
The deities we follow and love.

Earth Mother, mighty Kindreds,
Bless our steps this day, and uphold us even in adversity.

Children of the Earth,
Go in peace and blessings:
This service is ended.

Prayer for Peace

By Seamus

May there be peace in the North, in the East, in the South and in the West
May there be peace from above and below
May there be peace among us.
May the Ancestors remind us of our history and council our action and deeds.
May the Nature Spirits remind us of our responsibility, council our hearts and minds.
May the Shining Ones remind us of potential and council our thoughts and dreams.
May our work be in honor, service and balance.

Prayers to the Kindreds

Our Grove has always spoken from our hearts when it has come to the Kindreds: they always receive the finest words our tongues can offer, the most sincere statements of love our hearts can muster, and the deepest sincerity we can draw from within.

Often, we speak in prayer not only to one of the Three Kindreds, but to all of them at once: it is not only the gods and goddesses, the spirits of nature, or the mighty dead that we call out to. These prayers are some by our members that call to all the Kindreds, regardless of the "group" they may be in.

This first prayer is by the daughter of one of our Grove members, and it calls out to each Kindred, and draws on the imagery that appeals to her. There is sheet music at the end of this volume to go with this prayer, should one wish to sing it.

A Kindred Prayer

By Bess

To a log we set fire for the New Year to come,
For many mead pours as a blessing from some.
The drums beat in the background as the fire dances with the wind,
Invited are those from many hearth kins
Oh Shining Ones we offer a prayer

We walk with the old ones, the young and the new,
We retell their stories with mornings first dew.
The shadows hide secrets that heal our dear earth,
Our lessons we learned from their tears and their mirth
Oh Ancestors we offer a prayer

The children cheer and laugh while colored ribbons deck a pole,
Wild spirits come out to play lured from their winter holes.
To the trees they whisper, to the flowers they sing,
To the waters they tend and the life that it brings
Oh Landspirits we offer a prayer

This prayer, by Seamus, also calls out to each of the Kindreds, asking them to hear his voice and seeking their help in continuing to walk they path before him.

Kindred Prayer
by Seamus

To the Kindred three,
For all the blessings I thank thee
May my voice resound in the well.
May my voice echo through the trees.
May my voice carry on the fire.
I stand before you mighty, noble, ancient ones,
Not broken or on bent knee
But standing tall and free.
All that I am, is because of you.
May I walk in honor, balance, and service
May my actions be just,
My thoughts pure.
Hail and glory to the Kindred.

Prayers to Specific Ancestors

The following prayer was written atop the burial mound at Thermopylae in 2007, when our Grove Priest visited the battlefield.

Ancestor Prayer from Thermopylae
By Rev. Michael J Dangler

You inspire me.
I remember you.
I know your story.
Sleep in blessed rest.
Your duty is done.

Prayers to Specific Nature Spirits

It should come as no surprise to anyone that the Crane is highly honored within our Grove. To that end, we have several prayers that our members say to the Crane, including the ones in this section.

Garanus, to us, is the guardian and warder of our work, and our guide through life and ritual.

Garanus the Guardian

By Seamus

Garanus, crane-kin, guardian of my Grove
I call out to you today and ask that as I travel
Carry me on your wings, safely to my destination.
Hail Garanus!

The following prayer, a prayer to the Crane, the Grove's tutelary spirit, is designed for a gatekeeper prayer, but this is not the only way you can use it. It can simply be used to call upon Garanus whenever you need him.

A Prayer for Garanus

By Rev. Michael J Dangler

One foot in the water, Crane
One foot on land.
One eye in the blue sky, Crane
Always between.
The realms are your plaything
Ever your joy
Guide me through them this day
Old Ways I walk.
No one knows better, Crane
The ways between the worlds.

Prayers to Specific Shining Ones

Unlike the ritual invitations and invocations found in the next chapter, these are prayers to specific deities for specific things. These represent our personal relationships with the gods and goddesses, not our ritual relationships, necessarily.

Prayer for Strength (to various)

by Carmen

Epona, help my footing to be sure and my heart to be courageous,
Venus, help me to love myself and my mistakes, let me never be lacking in love for myself.
Diana, help my focus be true, and my intuition keen, and my drive precise.
Goddesses, I ask that you ensure me these gifts, guide my thoughts and actions, and allow me to see a part of you in me.

Prayer to Frigga, for Hospitality

By Anna Banana

Lady Frigga,
I thank you for your hospitality.
Yours is the home I can always rely on
When my own home is no longer true.
I thank you for the peace and the comfort you have given me,
And ask that you give me some to take on my way.
Help me to carry it like light inside of me,
That I may re-illuminate my own dark home.

Prayer to Agni

By Rev. Michael J Dangler

A friend to humankind:
Agni, bright fire.
A virtuous leader:
Agni, bright fire.
Liberal, giving priest:
Agni, bright fire.
Strong one, wishfulfiller:
Agni, bright fire.
He knows, but does not say.
He knows the first and last.
Ferryman through darkness,
Guiding us with his light.

Bright Belenos
By Seamus

Belenos, Bright Belenos
I call out to you tonight
Wrap me in your starry mantle
Protect me with your might
Illuminate my dreams,
until the coming of your light...

Seamus wrote this when faced with an impromptu visit from a very difficult person from his corporate office at work:

For Strength, from Tyr, Braggi, and Forseti
By Seamus

Tyr, give me the strength to hold my tongue and remember to sacrifice ego for the good of my family.
Forseti, give me the wisdom to think about the art of compromise and to think with a clear head.
Bragi, give me the inspiration to help my words to drip like honey.

Our Grove Priest, after being lost on the dangerous peaks of Mt. Olympus, had finally found his way back to the main trail as the sun was setting quickly.

A prayer to Zeus, in thanks for safe passage
By Rev. Michael J Dangler

For clear skies,
for keeping the rain off our backs,
for a safe journey on your mountain,
Olympian Zeus, be praised.
Look with favor on us as we return down,
look with favor on us as we return back up.
Olympian Zeus, be praised.

Prayer to Esus
By Rev. Michael J Dangler

Esus, guide me to cut the right branches,
to cut them the right length,

Prayer to Esus

By Anna Banana

I am but a sapling to you, patient Esus.
I am but a fawn that rests beneath your great trees.
I seek in you strength and serenity,
Purpose and vision,
Wisdom and peace.
Protect me as you have protected my mothers.
Counsel me as you have counseled my fathers.

Esus-Teutates,
As you guided me once,
Guide me again toward home.
and to cut them with the knowledge that I have to.

This, another prayer to Esus, is a prayer for comfort.

Prayer to Esus

By Rev. Michael J Dangler

Esus holds me when I cry.
Esus straightens my back.
Esus laughs with my joy.
Esus opens his arms
And I fall into them.

The next prayer, to Teutates, the "God of the Tribe," calls out for strength in a time of need. By calling to Teutates, we call out to the god that binds us all together as a single Grove.

Prayer to Teutates

By Rev. Michael J Dangler

Teutates, the way is difficult
Strewn with obstacles:
   Fear, doubt, and worry.
Help me to see that these obstacles
Are merely shells containing great treasures:
   Courage, Faith, and Peace.

This next is a prayer for Taranis, designed for use in a daily devotional, but it can also be used for a full ritual at the Summer Solstice or for rains.

Taranis

By Rev. Michael J Dangler

Thunderer, rolling across the sky
Driving the winds and the rains
Throwing your bolts and laughing
Loosing the waters upon the earth:
Taranis, without you the world does not grow.
I promise to you and offer to you tonight.

This prayer was written for Cernunnos, a god whose connections to the Ancestors and the tension between opposites is astounding.

Cernunnos Prayer

By Rev. Michael J Dangler
(heavily inspired by Ceisiwr Serith)

Cernunnos, sitting in the doorway,
Holding the opposites apart
Bringing the opposites together
Parting and uniting all things
Pouring out the wealth of the Otherworld
Fill me with knowledge
Unite all within me
Esti

Prayer to Cernunnos, Against Fear

By Anna Banana

Cernunnos,
Father of brave children,
Do not let fear stand in my way.
Guide me to find my own inner strength
And use it, honoring you with my deeds.

This is a prayer that can be said anywhere, anytime. It is a prayer for strength, guidance, and help when you don't know where else to turn. It is not written to any specific god or goddess, but is simply generic, calling out to whomever will help you.

Prayer to the Gods and Goddesses, for Strength

By Rev. Michael J Dangler

Uphold me, for I cannot hold myself.
Uplift me, for I have not the strength
Guide me, for I am lost without you.
I place full faith in you.
Hear my prayer,
Esti.

Weaver's Dream

By Kimberly Steffey-Rich

I wait for her silver toned call
The Morrigan
Celtic Mother, Raven Divine
Goddess Triune
I spin for her
bliss and burdens on spools
the Moon beckons full and bright
On the loom of Her hands
I weave my strands
fine silk strong as the wind
light as the flame that fires the cauldron
each thread a dream
each knot a memory
into the tapestry of life

Welcoming Math ap Mathonwy

By Aeryn

Greatest Mage, High Druid,
I call out to you,
Math ap Mathonwy,
Wisest of counsel,
Come warm yourself at my fire.
Grant to me the secrets of magic
And bless the worship I bring to you.
Great is the power that flows.
Many are your blessings, o Math!
For justice and knowledge,
For truth and ancient magics,
Math ap Mathonwy, accept my sacrifice!

Seasonal Prayers

As the seasons turn, we are often moved by their beauty to try and capture their progression in poetry and prayer. Sometimes, these two things come together in an astounding way, and lead to some of the most moving prayers spoken through the year. Here are some examples.

The Fires of Imbolc

Rev. Michael J Dangler

The fires of Imbolc have broken winter's back.
See again the blue skies.
See again the green grass.
See again the budding trees.
Though ice still may fall and bitter cold arise:
We are warmed by new life.
We are warmed by kinfolk.
We are warmed by returning sun.
The fires of Imbolc are within our hearts, brightly burning.

Three Cranes Grove
ADF
Columbus, Ohio

One of our members, Anna Banana, who has a deep gift of words, wrote this poetic prayer that draws on the joys of kinship and plenty, balanced by the reality of the harsh winter ahead. This payer reminds us that the Kindreds are here to sustain us through the winter and the hard times in our future, with love, kindness, and joy.

An Autumn Equinox Prayer

By Anna Banana

The last embers of summer will smolder long
Into the darkness of winter.
We will keep them in our hearts and feed them in our hearths
As we are drawn closer to our kin.
We seek warmth within each other and warmth within ourselves,
And warmth within our radiant gods.
We gather to praise our gods now.

Holy Ones, sustain us.
Nourish your children.
With the bounty of the harvest and the goodness of the Earth,
Nurture and protect us from the hunger of winter.

Let us be free from want.
Let us be free from fear.
Let us turn inward for strength and faith
And outward for the warm hospitality of others.

Ancient Ones, hear us.
Draw close to your children.
With our hearts full of love and our gratitude unending,
Let us honor you as worthy of sincerest praise.

Let us be blessed with virtue.
Let us be blessed with truth.
Let us turn toward you for strength and faith
Until they day our own winters descend
And we may share in the warm hospitality of your halls.

Each Beltaine, it is common for our Grove to celebrate the coming of summer. Most often, we celebrate this by calling to Belenus and Sirona: the sun king and the lady of the well. Here is a prayer for Gaimonios (the Gaulish name for Beltaine), followed by a prayer for Samonios (samhain). These prayers were written for the Liturgical Writing 1 course in ADF's Liturgist Guild Study Program.

Prayer to Belenus and Sirona: Giamonios

By Rev. Michael J Dangler

Belenos who shines above us
Sirona who wells from below
within us each your blessings meet
as into us your powers flow.
Drinking deep from shining waters
warming ourselves with light above
we stand before this godly pair,
and feel fulfilled with all their love.
Sunlight filtering from above
Waters flowing cool from the earth
between these two we stand complete
standing solidly, full of worth.
Within us mingle two powers:
Light shining on the waters now.
Love is made in leafy bowers
god and goddess showing us how.

Prayer to Cernunnos: Samonios

By Rev. Michael J Dangler

It is in you that the opposites meet
The balance of light and dark is no more.
The winter has come, fast and harsh, the heat
has left the world, and chilled it to the core.
The leaves, they fall and crinkle underfoot,
the sky cold grey, and nights they grow longer;
the tree's lost its sap, dug in with its root,
as first snows do fall, winter grows stronger.
Our hearth-fires burning, vig'rous at night
provide us with warmth, dispelling the cold.
Even in winter the world is alight
with all that we are: the brave and the bold.
Cernunnos, lord of liminality,
sit in our doorway, hold the worlds apart
accept from us this hospitality,
as we offer to the gods with our art.

Other Prayers

Shawneen's Flamekeeper Oath

By Shawneen

Brigid
Smith of my soul
Midwife to this life
Poetsinger of my songlines
My devotion, my service and my honor
To you Lady, I freely give.
Make of my life an offering
And burn away the things you know I do not need.
Temper me for the struggle and light my way in darkness.
Your flame, in love, I kindle.
May it ever serve as a beacon to the holy grace of your mantle.
Weave my thread into its weft of peace and protection.

This prayer was written for a ritual done by three Grove members who were, at the time, very new to the Grove. The ritual was to help heal the land, and was done at the Chadwick Arboretum on The Ohio State University campus, near the labyrinth there.

Prayer For the Renewal Of the Earth

By Anna Banana

Great Brighid, Child of the Good God, bringer of creativity and hope; we ask that you show us today not only your fires but also your source. May the cool, dark waters that feed your dancing flames flow through us, aiding us as we move to heal the land and comfort the land. Great Warrior, give us the strength to protect the vulnerable soil, and infuse the land with abundance, fertility, and the boundless miracle of creation. Spark the lives of tiny seeds to sow bright grasses and lush dark trees, and offer rain, fire-fed water, to nourish and gently heal. Beloved One, hear us! Bless this place and its people with your sacred gifts.

Janus is the deity most commonly associated with doors in Roman religion. He protects our homes from that which would bring harm to it or those within it. Not only is it a good idea to invoke Janus as a protector of the home, but Janus is also the gatekeeper between us and the realm of the deities, so establishing a good relationship with Janus may aid in enlisting his help in opening the gates in more elaborate rituals. It's not a bad idea to invoke him every time you enter and leave your home.
As you cross the threshold and close the door behind you, say:

Prayer When Leaving Home

By Rev. Jenni Hunt

Semper salve valeque, Jane Clusive
Greetings always, Janus, closer of doors!
Extend your hands in supplication and say:
Me absente te precor uti sis domum meam vigilans et ab injuria protegens.
I humbly beseech you to watch over my home in my absence, and protect it from harm.
Lock the door, then kiss your hand and touch this hand to the door, saying:
Ita est!
So be it!

Prayer Upon Returning Home

By Rev. Jenni Hunt

As you approach the entrance to your home, greet Janus, saying:
Salve Jane Patulci!
Greetings, Janus, opener of doors!
Extend your hands in supplication, saying:
Tibi gratias ago quod in me absentia domum meam vigilasti et ab injiria protexsti
Thank you for watching over my home in my absence and keeping it safe from harm.
Kiss your hand, touch this hand to the door, and unlock it, saying:
Gratias tibi ago!
I give you thanks!

Far-From-Home Prayer

Rev. Michael J Dangler

No matter where I am,
No matter how far,
No matter how long,
No matter how apart:
The Gods I worship are the Gods of my Tribe.
Teutates, you are here for me, and my worship is to you.
Hear my songs of praise this day.

To Thor, for Safe Travel

By Anna Gail

Hail Thor! Wielder of Mjollnir.
Defender of the Gods
God of the common Man.
Protect me as I walk the world this day
Keeping those that would cause me harm at bay

A Priest's Prayer

By Rev. Michael J Dangler

I have come to the place of sacrifice.
I pour oil upon the Fire.
I pour milk upon the Stone.
I bring silver to the Well.
I bring blessing to the Folk.
The heaven-bound boat is steered by my hand,
The priest of the people, the priest of the gods.

Guardian's Prayer

By Seamus

I stand firm with the Earth beneath me.
I stand tall with the Sky above me.
I stand strong with the Sea around me.
With the power of the Earth, Sea and Sky, I stand ready.
I am aided by the might of the Kindred
I am a guardian for this grove and stand ever vigil.

Prayer for the Empath
By Traci

Goddesses of compassion, of inner knowledge and emotions, hear me.
Brigid, Athena, Isis mothers of the empathetic soul, hear me.

I am thankful for the gifts you have given me.
Allow me to use my gifts to be a kind, gentle and caring soul.
Allow me to use my gifts to be understanding and compassionate
To those in need.

Also, I ask protection from the flood waters of emotion.
Protect my heart and mind from becoming too overwhelmed by the emotions of others.
Give me the knowledge to discern the difference between the thoughts and emotions
of my own heart and those of others around me.

Give me the ability to protect myself and find calm quiet center
when I am not acting as counselor.

Provide me courage as I listen to the trials of others
and calm my heart when I lay down to sleep.

Prayer for Inspiration before Negotiation
By Rev. Michael J Dangler

Ogmios, today I enter the fray
But I go not with sword or javelin,
shield or helm or coat of mail.
I go instead to this fight with my words,
clad in the armor of inspiration
a helm of awe upon my brow.
Guide me here today in my speech,
let it be tempered with vision,
strengthened by wisdom
and given authority by piety.
Let me speak as you speak,
and lead men with a silver chain
from my tongue to their ears.

Prayer for the Worrier
By Traci

Higher power of my heart, I come to you humbled and asking for aid.
I am troubled. Too much has caused my mind to fret.
I cannot sleep, I cannot focus.
I have allowed worry to consume my heart and thoughts.

I ask that you come to me and give me peace.
Allow me the understanding that my problems are temporary.
Remind me of the steady tree that bows in the wind, lest it break.

I ask for the patience to deal with each problem as it arises
and to admit I need help before I become overwhelmed.
I will try to remember to take challenges as they come and to bend
To the wind rather than allow it to break me.

Allow me the strength to deal with my problems before I lose control of them.
Please remind me of all the blessings you have already given me and know that I am
forever grateful.

Prayer for Fishes in an Aquarium
By Anna Banana

Thank you for living with me, little Kindred.
Your ways bring me wonder,
Your presence a smile.
My life would be emptier without you.

Prayer for a deceased Ferret
By Aeryn

Before the sun set today,
Your weasely soul crested the ninth wave.
May the wings of the crane carry you aloft
As you join the spirits of this place.
May your food ever be slathered with bacon grease,
May your hammock be slung from a stout branch,
And May the hours of your sleep always be at least twenty.
Hails!

This next prayer was meant to be read aloud quickly and rhythmically. It has a more playful, Wiccan feel. It might be entertaining for kids.
This prayer has also been published in Oak Leaves.

A Wild Thing's Prayer

By Anna Banana

thirteen chickadees trill on a trellis,
ringing out hymns to a sun-sung god.
sixteen bees make the hummingbirds jealous,
drinking all the honey where the mud-god trod.

sun-god, earth-god, trod and tread;
seven-tined antlers on the wild one's head.

the wren and the raven rasp chorus in a forest,
melodies mingling in a sweet discord.
red berry, yellow corn, yarrow and sparrow,
a mountain-top narrow where the hawk-lord soars.

hart-lord, hunt-lord, honey and mead,
seven-tined antlers on the wild-one's head.

churning and yearning, the sea tells his tale,
of death and rebirth and of seashells and shale.
the wolf stalks the deer and the winter stalks spring,
the old trees must perish so saplings may sing.

death-god, life-god, comfort and dread,
seven-tined antlers on the wild-one's head.

seven-tined antlers crown fearful and fair
the wild-one smiling on a wild thing's prayer.

Money Prayer
By Traci

Higher Power of my heart, again I come to you with humility and need.
I understand that money comes and goes. Today, though, I ask for enough.

Enough to cover my bills, to pay the debts that I owe and to allow me to free myself
from the worry of creditors.
Enough to provide for myself and my family, enough to provide all the daily needs we
have.

I am willing to work as I am able to provide, but times are tight. Please help me find
enough to make ends meet as you have in the past.

Remind me that generosity breeds generosity and that when my time of need is
through, that there are others than can benefit from my blessings.

Please help me to feel calm in knowing that I have always been provided for. I have
never wanted for anything and you have not come through. Please bless me with the
patience to wait until your blessings come to me,

I know you will provide.

Prayer for Work
By Rev. Michael J Dangler

As I set myself to work today,
Let my purpose be clear,
Let my mind be prepared,
Let my body be strong.
To the Kindreds I honor:
Ancestors, show me the way;
Nature Spirits, help me focus;
Shining Ones, bless my work.
Let all I do today reflect your blessings.
So be it.

A Prayer for Stupid Amounts of E-Mail

Rev. Michael J Dangler

A rushing waterfall confronts me,
Pouring forth, crashing down,
Overpowering my senses
And making me feel small.

Staring and feeling helpless,
Afraid of so much power,
Wondering where I fit
And simply not knowing.

But then I still myself,
Pausing and reflecting,
Focusing my attention
On a single drop cascading.

The drop travels down,
Small, alone, insignificant,
But vital to the whole
And vocal as the others.

Ogmios, as I face a deluge
Of modern communication and noise,
Help me to find the importance
Of each word and every sign.

Without the small parts
There is no whole.
The wonder of the deluge:
The parts that make it sing.

Obtaining a Job Interviewed For
By Rev. Michael J Dangler

When Lugh came to the gate, he was challenged:
"What art do you practice, what skill do you bring?"
Said Lugh, "A wright am I, a fixer of wheels."
"A fixer of wheels we have, we need you not."

Said Lugh, "A smith am I, a worker of steel."
"A worker of steel we have, we need you not."
Said Lugh, "A warrior am I, a champion famed."
"A champion famed we have, we need you not."

Said Lugh, "A harper am I, a singer of tunes."
"A singer of tunes we have, we need you not."
Said Lugh, "A hero am I, a man of great might."
"A man of great might we have, we need you not."

Said Lugh, "A wizard am I, a sorcerous man."
"A sorcerer we have, we need you not."
Said Lugh, "A leech am I, a knower of herbs."
"A knower of herbs we have, we need you not."

Said Lugh, "A bearer am I, who carries the cup."
"A cup bearer we have, we need you not."
Said Lugh, "A brazier I am, a worker of brass."
"A worker of brass we have, we need you not."

Said Lugh, "Is there one who knows every art you need,
One who is ideally fit for all things you want?"
Said the gatekeeper, "A man like that we have not,"
And he heralded Lugh to the king, and brought him inside.

Lugh of the long arm, many skilled and deeply talented,
Who interviewed at the door, and was granted the king's seat:
I raise my voice in praise to you and seek your favour.

Let it be known that none other can do what I can.
Let it be known that none other fits in this place.
Let it be known that none other has all my skills.
Let it be known that none other they have interviewed
is better able to do all the tasks that are required.

Lugh, shining god with the long arm,
This I pray to you.

Prayer for Work

By Rev. Michael J Dangler

Brigid, smith and poet:
Bless my tools that they may be ready today.
Lugh, skillmaster:
Bless my skills that they may shine today.
Ogma, honey-tongue:
Bless my voice that I may be understood today.
Grant inspiration, knowledge, and eloquence to me this day.
So be it.

Prayer for a Rough Work Day

By Rev. Michael J Dangler

I stand here and call out to those who have gone before:
Ancestors, who toiled to make ends meet;
Nature Spirits, who work to keep the world balanced;
Gods and Goddesses all, who hear our praises and prayers. . .

Today has been rough, a hard day.
Today has been frustrating, a tiring day.
Today has been frightening, a fearsome day.
Today has been crazy, a weird day.

At the end of the day, though, you remind me:
My family for whom I provide is here;
My friends with whom I relax are near;
Those who rely on my joy are here;
Those I turn to in need are near.

Today was just a day, and tomorrow will be another.
Through it all, though, I turn to you,
I rely on my friends and family,
And I know that I will make it through.

Ancestors, Nature Spirits, Shining Ones:
You give me strength and wisdom,
and I give you thanks.

This prayer was written the morning of Feb. 1, 2008, when our Grove Priest took a new day job. It is a prayer to Usas, the Vedic goddess of the dawn, for a new job, asking the blessings of a new dawn upon the person starting it. As with most prayers to Usas, it discusses her as the last of all dawns that came before her and the first of all to come: ever youngest and ever eldest.

Prayer for Beginning a New Job

By Rev. Michael J Dangler

Today dawns the last of all dawns that have been
And the first of all dawns that will be.
Clothed in light, she appears in the east
Awakening man and beasts and lighting the fires of sacrifice.
Beloved of heaven, Usas unveils the treasures hidden by darkness,
Distributing them to all the pious who make sacrifice.

Usas, you have awakened me to the last dawn and the first,
And though each glimpse of you wastes my life, it prolongs it yet again.
Bringer of wealth, breath of life, warder against evil:
Let this be the first of many days I greet in your blessed light.

Ritual Invocations

In each ritual, we call out to a number of spirits, powers, and Kindreds. These are some examples of evocations, invocations, and descriptive offerings we have used, organized by entity.

The Earth Mother

The Earth Mother is part of the core cult of ADF rituals, and one of two beings called to in our rituals that set ADF apart from so many other traditions (the other being the Gatekeeper). She is called many things, including Earth Mother, All-Mother, Mother of the Gods, Gaia, Nerthus, and a myriad of other titles and names.

She is an important goddess of the Neo-Pagan movement, regardless of whether she is an ancient deity or not, and regardless of whether a true "earth mother" appears in all mythologies. She is the first honored and the last thanked in any ADF ritual, for we are supported by her, nurtured by her, and bound to her in ways we cannot begin to fathom. She encompasses the cosmos in ritual, and she is all we know outside of it.

Our Grove has a long tradition of creative prayers to the Earth Mother. Here are some prayers we have used throughout the Grove's history.

This first prayer is an adaptation from a poem our first Grove Priest, Jenni Hunt, wrote:

Earth Mother Invocation
By Rev. Jenni Hunt

Feel her touch in the wind;
Taste her nectar in the air;
See her breath in the rippling water;
Smell her perfume in the trees and soil;
Hear her voice in the stones.

The Earth is her soul,
And Life is her prayer.
She is all there is,
And all there is is part of her.

Blessings to the All-Mother.

The Promise
By Seamus

Momma, I'm scared.
I know little one.
What will I eat?
Sister Rabbit will feed you.
What will I wear?
Brothers Deer and Bear with clothe you.
What if I'm cold?
Bother Oak and Sister Willow will burn bright for you.
Will I be alone Momma?
No my child, your brothers and sisters are everywhere. Listen to the wind sing through the trees, the laughter of the bubbling brook, in all my creatures there is a voice my child, listen with your heart not your ears...if you are lonely just look into the nighttime sky, and you will see Grandmother Moon smiling down on you, gaze onward and see your ancestors in the stars.
But Mamma. . .
No more buts little one, it is time for sleep, curl up into my bosom and let me warm you through the night. Someday you will grow to be the mightiest of all my children, and your children and their children. You must promise me that you will listen with your heart and help care for your brothers and sisters. They can teach you much but you must remember what they say. Teach your children the lessons of the forest and of the meadows. Teach them to love your Mother and all things big and small. . .
I will Momma, I promise. . .

Opening Prayer to the Mother of All
By Nate

Matrona, Ancestral Goddess and Great Mother of the Tribe, Great ancestress of all those here gathered. You came first and by rights receive the first honor. You who gave birth to the Gods and Goddesses. We invite you into this our Nemeton and pray that you bless and uphold our rite. So be it!

Earth Mother Prayer
By Anna Gail

Earth Mother
You who are sister, lover, mother
You nourish those that walk upon your breast
You embrace those that cry out to you
You are a comfort to those that seek you

Great All-Mother, your child loves and honors you
For your harvests to feed us, I thank you
For your colors to delight us, I thank you
For your slumber that we may be reborn each spring, I thank you
For your rebirth and renewed hope, I thank you

Earth Mother, Hail and thank you

Earth Mother Awakens
By Rev. Michael J Dangler

Boundless in blessings, the Earth Mother Awakens,
lifting her head from peaceful slumber,
covered in her quiet blanket of snow,
and dreaming of the greenery of spring.

She sighs a warm breath, warming her lover, the Sky.
As she stretches out, buds form on the trees,
animals come from their slumber, and the ground softens a bit.
Now all things are returning to life, in her joy.

Blessings on the Earth Mother.

Allmother Invocation 1.0

By Shawneen

Children of the Earth. . .
It is fitting that we begin by honoring the All Mother
She from whom we have all emerged.
She who sustains us
She to whom, in the fullness of time, our bones will return.
We honor her best by walking in balance.
We honor her best by keeping our footprints light.
Earth Mother, we ask that you ward and guard our rite.
All Mother, accept our offering.

Allmother Invocation 2.0

By Shawneen

Opening:

Children of the Earth. . .
It is fitting that we begin by honoring the All Mother
She from whom we have all emerged.
She who sustains us in this life.
She to whom, in the fullness of time, our bones will return.
Earth Mother, **ignite** your spark within us that we may know ourselves to be truly
human, truly holy and truly part of the web of life.
Support and sustain us
During this rite as you do throughout our lives
All Mother, accept our offering.

Closing:

All Mother, you have supported and sustained us. All that remains of these offerings
shall be returned to you.
All Mother, we thank you.

Earth Mother

By Rev. Michael J Dangler

From giant's flesh were you made
Springing from his sacrifice.
Your body was his body
Until it was portioned out.
You are abundant in height
And even broader in width.
You support us as we stand
And comfort us as we sleep.
We call to you, Earth Mother
For your blessings on this rite.

A Hittite Earth Mother Prayer

By Rev. Michael J Dangler
(heavily influenced by Harry Hoffner)

The Gods searched for her far and wide.
In green meadows and underbrush
In mud that stuck to their leg hair
In mountains and flowing rivers
In holy precincts the gods searched.
The Mother Goddess was found in
the forests that stretched about them
though she smiled and said she was
in all places they were searching.

Mother of us all, be with us:
This offering of pure honey
reminds us that the bees found you.

Ops Mater

By Rev. Jenni Hunt

Ops Mater. Goddess of the Bounty of Earth,
We send out words in praise of you, from whom all worlds flow.
Mystery of mysteries, this continual creation,
Like a fountain forever bubbling up from below
She is a cup that is never empty.
Generous One, eternally giving gifts,
We pray to you;
Ops Mater, we praise you.

Nerthus, Midnight Flame Festival 2008

By Rev. Michael J Dangler

On an island in the sea,
Within a sacred grove,
Your wagon awaits your ascension.

As the cows pull you forth,
War ends, swords are sheathed.
Quiet descends.

Nerthus, you move among us
Bathed in our joy for you.
Know our presence as we know yours.

Nerthus, accept our sacrifice.

Earth Mother Prayer (Spanish)

By Anna Banana

O madre amada de todo	O beloved Mother of All
De su matriz estrellosa la tierra verde brinca	From your starry womb the Earth springs
Usted que es el portador de toda la vida	You who are the bearer of all life
Rezamos que usted bendece y sostene este rito.	We pray that you bless and uphold this rite.
Madre de Todo, accepta nuestra ofrenda!	Mother of All, accept this offering!

Inspiration

As Druids, it is right that we should call on inspiration for our rituals. This is done in our Grove during the opening prayers, so that we may speak eloquently throughout the ritual.

Words in ritual are the link of communication between humans and deity. They are powerful, magical, and sacred. It is right that we should pray for good inspiration at each rite.

A common concept with inspiration is the idea of "Awen." Awen is a Welsh word that means "divine inspiration," and it is often conceptualized as a fire in the head. It is not the jumbled creativity of one who is inspired but not ordered; rather, it is the focusing of creative forces along a structured path. Poetry, music, and storytelling all fall into Awen. You might think of it as a classical muse, forming an idea within your head that you are then able to give life to.

Inspiration Invocation

By Rev. Michael J Dangler

I reach deeply within myself;
seeking, searching.
My eyes turn inward and see deep;
seeking, searching.
My fingers reach out, feeling forth;
seeking, searching.
My ears are open, listening;
seeking, searching.
My nose sniffs for any sign here;
seeking, searching.
My tongue tastes the sweet nectar now;
seeking, searching.
Here it is, within me, calling;
seeking, searching.
Here I am, to greet it, hold it;
seeking, searching.
Here we are, together, tightly;
holding, knowing.
Inspiration, I call to you;
hold me, know me.

Invocation to Apollo

By Rev. Jenni Hunt

Phoebus Apollo, bringer of light, son of
Zeus, the almighty, and Leto, the rich-haired, who
Bore him at Delos, where all manner of men now
Come bearing gifts, fine and fragrant for thee.

O Lord Apollo, who bears the gold sword, who
Shoots from afar with his bright silver bow;
Mighty slayer of dragons and lover of beauty;
Whose arrow strikes truer than Marsyas or Cupid.

Thou, who humbled the streaming, scheming Telphusa;
Whose lilting lyre delights all Olympus;
Whose oracle utters Zeus's unerring will;
Whose art, aim, and intellect reigns supreme over all.

Sweet-tongued Apollo, who sings for the Gods, may'st thou
Guide thence our praises to bathe them in honor;
For we are but mortals, and thou art a God;
Only this boon we beg thee, grant to us now:

That our voices be pleasing to Gods, Spirits, and Manes;
That the aim of our rite strike its target precisely;
That our blessings and theirs pass freely between
The realms of the Kindreds and the lips of our Seer.

The following prayer is one you can say in work situations when you need to watch what you say, or be political.

Bragi Prayer

By: Seamus

Bragi…Odinson.
Bragi…with your tongue of gold,
Bragi…best of bards,
Bragi…let your inspiration flow!

Inspiration Invocation

By Shawneen
(used at Imbolc 2008)

Brigando,
Our Smith, Our Healer, Our True Poet,
We are triple blessed by the shining flame of Our Hearth
Give us the Fire in our Heads,
Give us the Fire in our Hearts,
Give us the Fire for our Voices,
That our praise may arise upon your Good Fire!
That our voices may resound in your Holy Well!
Thrice and together we chant the holy Awen
AHHHHHHHWOOOOOOENNNNNN (x3)
At Winters Hinge
Bíodh sé amhlaidh!

Inspiration

By Rev. Michael J Dangler

Snow and ice have cooled our minds
Cold winds have blown away our fertile thoughts
Silent nights have stilled our tongues
Like the bear, the fox, and the toad
Our creativity hibernates without the warmth of the sun.
Come to us now, Inspiration, as the sun returns!
As the sun grows in strength
So may the fire in our hearts!

Inspiration

By Shawneen

Powers of inspiration
We call to you and ask that you attend our heart shrines.
Grant us the Poets' Fire. . .
That our voices may resound in truth and in beauty;
That our actions may flow in power and with grace;
And so our rite may connect us. . . to each other and to the Mighty Kindreds!
Let us bring our voices together as a Grove and chant the Holy AWEN three times:
AWEN AWEN AWEN

Awen Inspriation Prayer (Spanish)

By Anna Banana

Poder de inspiración que ayuda a nosotros
Voz del fuego de la sabiduría
Voz del pozo de inspiración
Entra la santuario de nuestros corazones
O! Entra la santuario de nuestros corazones
Nos permita saber de todas las cosas buenas o malas
Guía nuestro rito con la verdad
Le llamo a usted que nos de un corazón claro
O poder de inspiración en este lugar sagrado
O poder de inspiración durante este tiempo sagrado
Lo hace!

[translation of Awen Inspiration Prayer]

Power of inspiration that attends [helps] us
Voice of the Fire of Wisdom
Voice of the Well of Inspiration
Enter the sanctuary of our hearts

Oh! Enter the sanctuary of our hearts
Let us know of all things, good or bad
Guide our rite with the truth
We call upon you to give us a clear heart

Oh power of inspiration in this sacred place
Oh power of inspiration in this holy time
So be it!

Call for Inspiration

By Rev. Michael J Dangler

From deep within us,
A cauldron bubbles.
We reach our hand into it,
Draw our hand to our lips
And drink deeply of our inspiration.
Let us be filled with eloquence and creativity this day.

Inspiration Prayer
By Anna Banana

Radiant Brighid, goddess of golden mantle and bright eye, lady of knowing smiles and hands that cherish any craft! You who are smith and healer, warrior and poet, patroness of the inspired... hear us! We call to you now and open our hearts to your sacred flame.

Kindle in us your three great fires: that of the hearth, that of the forge, and that of the heart. Illuminate our minds and guide our tongues that we may speak with reverence, truth, and skill. Let our words be the poetry of ancient wisdom rising from glistening embers. Let our minds be tempered with wisdom, focus, compassion, and the bard's gift. Hear us, Shining Brighid!

Call to Inspiration
By Tamie McKenna

Powers of Inspiration:
We ask in firth through moderation
that this High Day of Imbolc be nurtured in piety.
Through your vision may all our thoughts, words and deeds
be in wisdom along this path of integrity.
With the courage to persevere when hospitality is denied
guide us to find fertility in inspiration
when honoring the Holy Ones.

Powers of Inspiration enjoy this honor and accept our sacrifice.

Gatekeeper

The Gates and the Gatekeeper are the second part of the core cult of ADF practice. Most Groves call on a deity for a Gatekeeper, and occasionally our Grove will as well. We are more likely, however, to use an heroic nature spirit, Garanus, the Crane, who is our tutelary spirit in this Grove.

Primarily, the Gatekeeper should be a being that is liminal already, someone who is already between the worlds and who can help you to turn the sacred center we establish in ritual into a center that is connected to all the worlds and realms. A Gatekeeper should be someone with whom you have a positive relationship, who will help you with little argument and certainly with understanding of the process. The being best used is probably good-natured and that you trust.

Gatekeepers in ADF ritual are not beings you should need to fight with, trick, or best in a riddle contest. Deities are best for this because they certainly have dominion between the worlds. Probably the quintessential Gatekeeper is the Vedic

73

Agni, or the Roman Ianus. These are gods who are very strongly connected to humans and also to the gods. Agni, for instance, is born when he is kindled, and is practically an open Gate as soon as the wood starts to smoke. An open door lets Ianus in, and what better way to call to mind a gate than the action of opening a door?

Ancestors can be used, as well, if that ancestor is an heroic ancestor. Ancestors themselves are not liminal, and the restless dead (the only kind of actually liminal dead) are not trustworthy enough in general. They fall under "outdwellers." But someone like Orpheus, Heracles, or other great heroes might work very well. The important thing is an established "friend of humans" and "welcome among the gods" sort of liminality.

As for nature spirits, it is an amusing little point of contention. In general, they do not fit well: most are tied to this realm alone, and you do not hear of many that cross realms; however, as with the ancestors, an heroic nature spirit would do very nicely.

Our Grove's relationship with the Crane as a Gatekeeper in many rites is unique, so far as we know. We have defined him as a being of many realms and many worlds, and over time, Garanus (the improperly declined name we use for the Crane) has become an heroic Nature Spirit, especially within our conception. In our evocations, we describe him as "sleeping on land, feeding in the waters, and flying in the sky; existing in all worlds and beholden to none." Adding to that, we have taken the crane's migration pattern, and we also indicate that the crane flies "beyond the seas," which is a traditional location for the Otherworld. In this way, we have mythologized the very concrete aspects of the normal, run-of-the-mill animal and he has become heroic for our Grove.

Garanus, then, is the Grove's primary Gatekeeper: our relationship with him is long and loving, and it is certainly solid. Though his name is Gaulish, the Crane exists in all the hearth cultures of ADF as a bird of mystery and liminality, and can be used for any Grove rite.

Call to the Gatekeeper
Standard, tweaked ADF wording

Garanus,
You who stand between the realms,
Open the ways for us.
Guide us as we walk in your holy ways,
Guide us as we walk the Sacred Road.
Share your magic with us,
Ward us as we travel to meet the Kindred.
Garanus, accept our sacrifice!

This evocation is to Ianus, the Roman god of beginnings and opening doors.

Evoking Ianus

By Rev. Jenni Hunt

Salve Ianus Pater!!
Ianus Inceptio, God of beginnings;
Ianus Brifons, Two-faced Ianus;
Ianus Patulcius, Opener of doors;
Ianus Domesticus, Protector of homes;
Ianus Quirinus; God of the folk:
Lend wings to our prayers and conjure a portal between us and the world of the Gods.
Through your door, let the prayers of your supplicants pass to the Kindreds.
IANUS PATER, MACTE HOC SACRIFICIO… Ianus Pater, accept our offering!

This is a slightly longer prayer to Ianus, used in our Saturnalia rites when Ianus is the Gatekeeper. We have always spoken it in both English and Latin, and the use of the Latin is fairly important to the calling.

Invocation to Janus (from Ovid's Fasti, I. 63-72)

Two-headed Janus, opener of the softly gliding year,	*Iane biceps, anni tacite labentis origo,*
who alone of the shining ones beholds his own back,	*solus de superia qui tua terga vides,*
Bless our leaders, whose cheerful toil	*dexter ades ducibus, quorum secura labore*
provides peace to the fruitful earth, peace to the sea.	*otia terra ferax. otia pontus habet:*
May you bless the leaders, the folk and the people of Quirinus	*dexter ades patribusque tuis populoque Quirini,*
and by your nod, open the temples white.	*et resera nuto candida templa tuo.*
A propitious light arises: attend with a breath of silence.	*Prospero lux oritur: linguis animisque favete!*
Now must good words be spoken on a good day.	*nunc dicenda bona sunt bona verba die.*

Invitations to the Ancestors

This prayer was written at Samhain 2007 and offered up in our public ritual as a praise for the Ancestors.

Ancestor Prayer
By Rev. Michael J Dangler

When you were born,
The earth became your body,
The stone became your bone,
The sea became your blood,
The sun became your eye,
The moon became your mind,
The wind became your breath.

When you passed to the Otherworld,
Your breath became the wind,
Your mind became the moon,
Your eye became the sun,
Your blood became the sea,
Your bone became the stone,
Your body became the earth.

When we were born, you did the same for us:
You called forth the earth and rocks;
The sea arose and the sun descended;
The moon shone down and the winds sang.
For those who come after, we shall do as you did for us
When we are gone, we shall do as you did before.

Ancestors, we honor you.

Ancestor Invocation

By Seamus

Cattle die, kinsmen die,
you yourself must likewise die,
but word-fame never dies
for him who achieves it well.
Cattle die, kinsmen die,
you yourself must likewise die,
but one thing that never dies
the verdict on each man dead.
Lo do I see the faces of my fathers,
Lo do I see the faces of my mothers,
The faces of my ancestors stretch out before me
And I hail my Afar and Disir and thank you for your sacrifices.
Ancestors I welcome to my fire, meet me at the boundary,
Guard and ward me as I walk the elder ways.
Ancestors accept my sacrifice.

Ancestors Invocation

By Rev. Jenni Hunt, for the Unity Rite at Three Realms, 2006

The Children of the Earth call out to the Mighty Dead:
Hear us, O, Ancestors:

You pioneers, who bravely explored new lands, mapped the world and built roads that
we may now find our way to each other.
You entrepreneurs, who plowed the boundaries of new settlements, planted our hearths
and domesticated the wild plants and animals that live with us and sustain us.
You teachers, who convey to us the wisdom of the ages, the lessons you learned the
hard way, and who instruct us in the ways of ghosti.

Come to our fire, Ancestors;
Meet us at the boundary;
Guide us and ward us as we walk the elder ways.
Ancestors, accept our offering.

Ancestors Invitation

By Rev. Michael J Dangler

The Children of the Earth call out to the Mighty Dead.
Hear us, our Ancestors, our Kindred.

To those who followed ancient paths shrouded in darkness,
lighting torches for those who came after:
You offered the first sacrifice,
Received the first cup of blessing,
And worked the first great work.
We offer you welcome.

To the dead who held this land sacred,
whose feet trod ancient and winding paths:
Upon your hearts are the blessings of this land,
With your hands you applied those blessings,
And with your memory we may access them again.
We offer you welcome.

To those whose faces appear in joyful memory,
tied to us in tradition, in joy and in love:
You hold our hands as we seek knowledge,
Reveal to us the blessings of the world around us,
And lead us down the torch-lined path.
We offer you welcome.

Ancestors, we call to you:
We may not know all your names,
But your names are known to the fire in the mound,
And we call out with that fire in our hearts.

Come to our fire, Spirits
Meet us at the boundary
Guide us and ward us as we walk the elder ways.

Ancestors, accept our sacrifice!

Ancestor Prayer
By Anna Gail

Mighty Dead hear our call,
You who are our Ancestors, our Chosen Kindred
We Hail you.
You who have fought before us,
We Hail you.
You who have sacrificed before us,
We hail you.
You who have laughed before us,
We Hail you
You who have cried before us,
We Hail you.

Come to our fire, Spirits
You Elders that have blazed the trail we now tread,
Meet us at the boundaries
Join us as we honor the old ways.

Ancestors of the blood we honor you
Ancestors of the People we honor you
Ancestors of the Land we honor you
Ancestors, accept our offering.

Ancestors

By Seamus

We call out to the ancestors.
We stand here in our place in time
Not the beginning, nor the end
Just another face in line

To the ancestors of blood and bone
Whose hearts beat with ours.
Whose words echo in our hearts
We welcome you.

To the ancestors of dirt and stone
Whose footsteps mark this earth
Whose words echo in the trees
We welcome you.

To the ancestors of time untold
Whose lessons we hope to learn
Whose words echo in ours minds
We welcome you.

Ancestors of those gathered, of the land and of the folk.
We ask that you meet us at boundary, join us at our fire
Aid and ward us as we walk the elder ways.
Ancestors accept our sacrifices.

Invitations to the Nature Spirits

A Winter Nature Spirit Prayer
By Rev. Michael J Dangler

A child of the earth calls out to the spirits of this place
Hear me, spirits of nature!
Though it is cold outside
And many of you sleep beneath the ground
Or in nests high above my head,
I ask that you hear my voice,
And join your call to mine
As I call the sun back to the skies
To bring her warmth and shining love
For all of us to feel.
Welcome, and thanks to the Nature Spirits!

Nature Spirits Invocation
By Anna Banana

You who inspire us with majesty:
The towering mountain and the stag in the wood.
You who instruct us with simplicity:
The single earth-worm dancing in the dirt.

You who are the spirits of Nature that surround and support us
With wisdom and grace;
We call to you now and say welcome
Here in this time and here in this place.

You are the joy of the seasons,
The wildness that sings always in our blood.
You are the fleeting glimpse of freedom incarnate
And the faithful companion at our side.

Nature Spirits,
You who fly and swim and run and climb and crawl and wriggle—
We welcome you!
Accept this sacrifice!

Invitation to the Nature Spirits
By Rev. Michael J Dangler

The Children of Earth call out to the Spirits of this Land.
Hear us, companions and teachers!

Though it is cold outside,
and many sleep beneath the earth
or in nests above our heads,
wrapped tightly in long winter's sleep:
Know that we honor you here today!

Spirits of this place,
who were here long before us,
who ask who it is we are:
Know that we honor your presence,
we remember that we are guests.
We offer you welcome.

Spirits of growing green,
whose shoots peek out in wonder,
asking: is it our time?
Know that the earth welcomes you,
and the folk anxiously await your arrival!
We offer you welcome.

Spirits who guide us,
who move between realms
and challenge us to grow with them:
Know that we remember your aide
and that we keep our bargains with you.
We offer you welcome.

Come to our fire, Spirits;
Meet us at the boundary.
Guide and ward us as we walk the elder ways.

Nature Spirits, accept our sacrifice!

Land Spirits
By Seamus

We call out to the land spirits.
We stand in our place in line
Not above, below or outside
But within the circle of life

To the spirits of dirt and stone
To the earth that holds our bones
Earth-kins we welcome you.

To the spirits of shrub and tree
To all things growing and green
Green-kins we welcome you.

To the spirits of fur and fin
To the creatures of feather and skin
Animal-kin we offer you welcome

Nature spirits of the earth, green and animal kins
We ask that you meet us at the boundary, join us at our fire
Aid and ward us as we walk the elder ways.
Nature Spirits accept our sacrifices.

Wellspring Nature Spirit Prayer
By Rev. Michael J Dangler

Dirt on my pants
Honey bees that visit
Bullfrogs that sing
Apple blossoms we smell
Grasses that we roll in
Dandelions we crown our gods with
Mosquitoes we dodge and slap
Oaks whose bark is rough
and leave their traces in our hair.
Nature Spirits who are always there,
If only we can see you,
Accept our Welcome!

Nature Spirits Invitation
By Jan Krueger

The Children of the Earth call out to the Nature Spirits!
Hear us, Allies and Guides!

To those spirits who crawl or stride:
Patient Turtle, Bounding Doe.
To those spirits who burrow or slide:
Cautious Mole, Cunning Serpent.
Come, and Be Welcome!

To those spirits who flit or fly:
Buzzing Bee, Sharp-Eyed Hawk.
To those spirits who swim or dive:
Glittering Gills, Darting Fins.
Come, and Be Welcome!

To those spirits who climb and grow:
Blooming Flower, Creeping Vine.
To those spirits who ripple and flow:
Shining Lake, Rushing Stream.
Come, and Be Welcome!

Come, Spirits of this Land,
And join us at the fire.
Mix your magic with ours,
And Meet us at the Boundary.
Guide us and Ward us as we walk the Elder Ways.

The Children of the Earth call out,
Nature Spirits, Accept our Offering!

Invitations to the Shining Ones

Invitation to the Deities
By Rev. Michael J Dangler

The Children of Earth call out to the Shining Ones.
Hear us, eldest and brightest!

To all the gods and goddesses,
First children of the Mother
who honor her as we do you today:
Know that we sing your praises
and that we tell your stories.
We offer you welcome.

Gods and goddesses of those here gathered,
you who walk with us down these paths,
who offer us shelter from the storm:
Know that we hold you in our thoughts
and that your blessings lift our souls.
We offer you welcome.

Deities of this place,
Old ones who are tied to this land,
whose voices are the song that rises from it:
Know that we walk here in balance,
and pray that we honor you well.
We offer you welcome.

You bring us the waters that bless our lives:
When we drink of the waters,
we remember that you have fought for them on our behalf,
and we are grateful.

Come to our fire, Shining Ones;
Meet us at the boundary.
Guide and ward us as we walk the elder ways.

Deities, accept our sacrifice!

Shining Ones Invocation

By Seamus

Hail the Shining Ones,
The Gods of this place.
Those who have walked this land
Whose voice is on the wind
Those whose hearts beat in the land
We offer you welcome
To the Matrons and Patrons
Of those gathered here
Whose voice is in our ear
Whose hearts beat with ours
We offer you welcome
To all the Shining Ones
Whose gifts light the community
Whose voices rise up in chorus
Whose heartbeats mark all time
We offer you welcome

Shining Ones Invocation (Norse)

By Anna Banana

The children of the Earth call out to the Shining Ones!
Hear us, Aesir and Vanir!
You who have given us body and spirit,
Sense and courage, heart and health,
Well have you crafted your children
Who welcome you now with limitless thanks!
Eldest and Mightiest, Patrons and Place-Gods,
Bringers of blessing and teachers of runes,
You who have taught us of faith and of honor
Of troth and right virtue,
We call to you now!

Join us, o powerful dwellers of Asgard—
Accept this sacrifice!

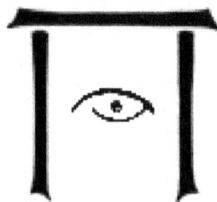

This is half prayer, half toast to the Shining ones, spoken at the Sumbel at Wellspring in 2007:

Sumbel Prayer

By Rev. Michael J Dangler

From far or near,
Within or without,
bringing us the mead of inspiration,
gazing upon us as friends and family and lovers.
Hail the Shining Ones!

Calling the Shining Ones

By Rev. Michael J Dangler

Our voices ring out among the trees,
lifted by the fire's warmth,
resounding in the depths of the well.

We reach out our hands,
filled with gifts of love and joy,
and offer to the deities.

Their hands reach out to ours,
fingertip brushing fingertip,
as they receive our gifts.

When their hands reach out, though,
they reach out not only to receive,
but also to give in reciprocity.

No hand that reaches out is empty,
either in gift or in blessing.
Such is the way of you Shining Ones.

Hear our call, Shining Ones:
join us here,
and receive our gifts so we may give again.

Shining Ones, accept our sacrifice!

Invitations to Other Kindreds

The Kindreds are not only to be found in the division of "Ancestors, Nature Spirits, and Deities." They may also be divided according to location, or function, or many other things. Here is one example, used in the Grove's Druid Moon Rites, of different Kindred invitations.

Calling to the Upper Kindreds

High in the Heavens, Heroes and Holy
Beyond the visible reaches of the Sky
Beyond the Veil of the Stars and Sun
Those Kindred that shine with light from Above
Shining Ones, Ancestors, Nature Spirits
Far-Seeing and Brightly clothed in gold light
Come to my Fire, offerings for Thee
A welcome to the Powers of Heaven
Be comfortable in my abode tonight.

Calling to the Middle Kindreds

Here among us are Gods and Dead and Sidhe
Standing within mists, coming to meet us
Coming nearer as we give offering
Standing next to us in our times of need.
In trees and streams, under foot, in the air
The Spirits of Place surround us always
Their songs reach our ears, their beauty our eyes
I call welcome to Spirits of this Realm
Be comfortable in my abode tonight.

Calling to the Chthonic Kindreds

Down below our feet, deep within the ground
In the fertile womb of the Earth Mother
Are denizens of Dark, unknown to us:
Gods of the Earth, Ancestors, and Earth-Kin.
Our bones will rest here though our soul will rise
Now we pour libation to these Kindred
Knowing their place in life and the Cosmos
I welcome the spirits of Dark Earth.
Be comfortable in my abode tonight.

Key Offerings

The Key Offerings are usually individual prayers of praise to deities (though they do not necessarily have to be to deities only). These are the climatic offerings to the beings of the occasion in any ritual. This is a prayer to Garanus, designed to be used with a drumbeat that follows the syllable count.

Calling Upon the Crane

By Rev. Michael J Dangler

Garanus Crane,
Totem of Tribes
Guide of our Folk,
We call to you.

Garanus Crane,
Warder of Ways,
Keeper of Gates,
We call to you.

Garanus Crane,
Trav'ler through Worlds,
Joy of our Hearts,
We call to you.

Garanus Crane,
Singer of Songs,
Holder of hands,
We call to you.

One foot on land,
One foot in sea,
Eye to the sky,
We call to you!

Garanus Crane,
Sacrifice made,
Hearts open wide,
We call to you!

Anna Banana wrote this invocation in 2005, and we've been more-or-less using it since.

Cernunnos Invocation (for Samhain)
By Anna Banana

Listen to the silence of the Earth beneath you.
Listen to the pause at the bottom of each breath.
Know the fragility of life and accept it:
And rejoice, for even in the dark it endures.

We raise our voices now beyond the circle of our fire,
Beyond the embers of autumn's faint glow.
We call to the listening darkness of Winter,
And to the God who will guide us as we step into its shade.

Cernunnos,
Antlered God of Threshholds!
Keeper of the Gates of Death!
You Who are Terrible, Merciful, Liminal,
You are the Guardian of the Realms Beyond!
We ask that you carry our voices to the Ancestors
That we may honor them with courage and love;
We ask that you bless us with strength and with virtue,
That we may persevere even through fear.

Cernunnos,
God whose gift is Equilibrium!
Ruler of Death yet Protector of Life!
You Who hold all opposites apart,
You in Whom all opposites are united:
Teach us the wisdom of balance
That we may find warmth in the winter
And hope in the dark.

Cernunnos, Lord,
God at the Center,
Come to our Fire
That your worship be known.

Prayer to Hela

By Anna Gail

Daughter of Lopt
Mistress of the honored dead
Walker between two worlds:
Life and Death
Each feeding off the other
Each necessary for the existence of all

Mysteries within your eyes
Knowledge within your mind
Keeper of the dead
You who have been given dominion over the realms
Your face downcast for the burden you hold
And the loss of those you loved

You are the hail, Hagalaz
You are the seed that feeds life from death
Guarder of Graves
Éljúðnir is your hall, the entrance is Stumbling block
Your dish is Hunger, the knife is Famine
Your bed is Sick-Bed and the curtains Gleaming-bale

Sister to the wolf and serpent
Punisher of evil, to Nastrand those go
Deliverer of judgement
Companion to Baldr
Walker between two worlds
Life, death: Hope, despair

Lady of light and dark,
Guardian of the souls of ancestors
~ Hail!

This next prayer, a call to Odin, is inspired by the stanza for Anzuz in each of the three rune poems. The first two lines of each stanza repeat the line from the rune poem, and then comment on the poem as part of the prayer.

Odin invocation and mead offering
By Tanrinia

The children of the Earth call out to Odin

"Aged Gautr, and prince of Asgard
Lord of Valhalla" -- All Father
From Ask and Embla's first breath
To Ragnarok's end
We call to you

"The way of most journeys, but a scabbard of swords"
Grey wanderer, traveler
Chooser of the slain, and leader of the Host
Death bringer and light father
We call to you

"Source of all language, pillar of wisdom
A comfort to wise men -- a blessing and joy to every king"
Winner of runes and mead and vision
Bringer of the madness and passion of inspiration
We call to you

We offer that which you gave
That you may have or share as you will
In thanks and gratitude we make this offering

HAIL ODIN!

This next prayer is a prayer to Taranis, the Thunderer of Gaulish mythology. It is designed to read like the sound of arriving, present, and retreating thunder.

Taranis

By Rev. Michael J Dangler

Thunderer,
in far-flung reaches of the heavens.
Clouds, rolling in and around,
your rumbles reaching our ears,
and we tremble at the sound.

Thunderer,
nearing our home and our lands
bringing storms and rain and light,
covering the world in storm-clouds.
Standing on our side, win us this fight.

Thunderer,
retreating from we who are left whole,
our land now knows your terror,
but your mighty terror defends us.
Taranis, Thunderer, none fairer.

The next pair of prayers, one to Belenus and one to Sirona, was used at our Beltaine Rite in 2007.

Invocation to Sirona

By Anna Banana

Sirona, Lady of the Flowing Waters,
Hear my words as they resound in the Well!
Yours is the supple movement of the dark waters that course beneath the land,
And the murmur of cool sweet rivers
That wash away exhaustion
And bring forth life.

Sensuous One,
You pull the heavy robes of winter off the land
And expose the potential within us.
You teach us of strength in vulnerability
And delight in uncertainty and hope.

Sirona,
As you caress the lands and encourage the erotic blossoming of life,
Bring us a sensual and prosperous summer
And heal away the scars that winter has wrought.

Bless us with pleasure, freedom, and fertility
As we bless you in turn and show you our love.
Goddess Sirona!
We dress your Well
Where the Earth opens up to the Sky.

Lady Sirona,
bless and renew us!

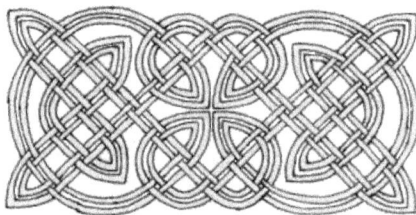

Belenus Invocation

By Anna Banana

Belenus, Lord of the Radiant Sun,
Hear my words as they arise on the fire!

Yours is the glittering movement of stars
And the heat of the noon-day sun on our faces;
You are the Quickener of Life,
The Blossomer of Flowers and Opener of Seeds.

Powerful One,
Your awaken the world from slumber
And bid it to dance in your light.
You expose that which was hidden
And allow it to thrive in unrestrained joy.

Belenus,
As you stir the sap in the trees,
Stir the sap within us as well.
Awaken us to our potential and allow for new, beautiful growth.

Bless us with freedom from fear and want
As you shower us in your generous light,
Knowing that we bless you in turn,
Thanking you for the spark of life.

Belenus,
Bless and awaken us!

This payer is also written for Belenus. It was used first in our Summerset 2005 ritual.

Belenus Prayer

By Rev. Michael J Dangler

Belenus, Sun King!
Hear my words as they arise on the fire!
From your fire comes our internal flame!
From you comes warmth and love!
We ask your blessings be upon us,
Ever increasing,
As we raise our voices to you!

Belenus, whose starry mantle shines in darkest night,
Bring forth within us the hidden inspiration we seek;
Draw the inspiration out. Order it with your shining light!
Belenus, give us Inspiration!

Belenus, who is the sun, draw your bright chariot across the sky:
Warm us with the bright glow of fellowship,
Bring us together to revel in your brilliant light!
Belenus, give us Fellowship!

Belenus, whose divinity is blinding, whose gifts cannot be fathomed;
Show us your generosity, born from our long relationship,
From old bargains kept. Shine your blessings upon us!
Belenus, give us Blessings!

Belenus, Lord of Light!
Hear the intentions of our hearts
As they are lifted to you
By the fire's vigor!

Belenus, give us your light!

Prayer of Sacrifice to Teutates

By Rev. Michael J Dangler

Teutates, each of us comes before you, a sacrifice of mistletoe in our hand, our hearts full of praise for you.

Our hearts have sung your praises, and our hands have offered sacrifice. Now, we bring forth the mistletoe, our highest crown, an outgrowth of us all. We have harvested it with care, for it contains all that is best in us. This is our offering to you: that which is best in us, and best in the Grove.

We gather around the fire, close together, a Grove whose branches and roots entwine, each of us rooted deep and crowned high.
Teutates, God of the Tribe, known to us in many ways, guiding us for all our days:

> The People of Three Cranes call out to you!
> Hear our words as they arise on the fire!
> Hear our voices as they resound in the well!
> To you we make this sacrifice, Teutates!

> The Mistletoe, the All-Heal, and all that is best in us.
> Teutates, accept this Sacrifice!

Prayers of Sacrifice

As each of us makes sacrifice, we often find ourselves wishing to speed the offerings we have made on to the Otherworld with our voices. These prayers help do that. This first was written to be spoken or chanted as an offering of oil is poured out upon the fire.

Fire of Sacrifice

By Rev. Michael J Dangler
(from a prayer by Ceisiwr Serith)

> Fire of Sacrifice,
> You burn the offering
> Making it fit for Gods
> And all the Holy Ones.

To Agni, for the Final Sacrifice

By Rev. Michael J Dangler

Agni, your voice sings when you devour the sacrifice!
Transform it now, distribute it to the gods you have brought!
Visit each in their place upon the sacrificial grass,
and show them the piety of their worshippers this day!
Agni, accept our sacrifice!

Prayers for Divination

Often, we find it useful to pray for knowledge before seeking omens, whether our method be runes, ogham, or augury. Here is one possible divination prayer that the Grove has used.

Runic Divination Prayer

By Ceisiwr Serith
(adapted for runes by Rev. Michael J Dangler)[5]

Speak to me as you follow the wind,
tiles of ash within my hand.
Follow perfectly the waves of the air-ocean,
making known to me their invisible pattern.
Out of the Well of the Wyrd they flow,
Carrying the wisdom that is their gift.
Carry it to me also, give to me, ash spirit,
the knowledge that you have,
the knowledge that we seek.

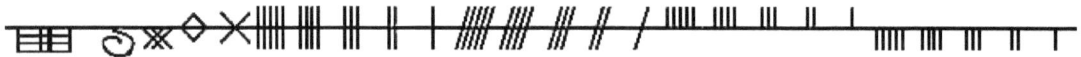

---

[5] This prayer was originally written for oracular work, but it fit so beautifully with runes that some modifications were made to the text and it flowed beautifully from there.

Seer's Prayer Before the Omens Are Taken

By Shawneen

We have offered to the Holy Ones,
We have honored the Mighty Kindreds;
Now let us open to them.
We look for the returning flow of energy as is our ancient bargain,
Standing in the center of our Sacred Grove we ask:
Have our sacrifices been accepted?
And we ask:
What do the Shining Ones offer to us in return?
And we ask:
What further needs do the Kindreds have of us?

Piacular Offering

Piacular offerings are made after the final offering, and are designed to ensure the completeness of the ritual. The offering is made to all the Powers, in the event that something was forgotten or left undone (or, possibly, done incorrectly).

Piacular Offering

By Rev. Jenni Hunt

Patron of this Rite,
Gods and Goddesses,
Holy Ancestors,
Spirits of this place:
If anything we have done here has offended you,
If anything we have done here has been incomplete,
If anything we have done here has not been in the proper manner,
Accept this final offering in recompense.

Outdwellers

One classification of Kindreds that we rarely speak of is the Outdwellers, forces that stood against our Gods, forces of Chaos, and forces that cannot harmonize with our work. For them, offering prayers to keep them away are often written.

Outdwellers Challenge

Rev. Michael J Dangler

First came Sigi, son of Oðin;
Then came Rerir, son of Sigi;
Then came Volsung, son of Rerir;
Then came Sigmund, son of Volsung;
Then came Sigurðr, son of Sigmund.
It was Sigurð who would slay the serpent.

The serpent held the Otter's Ransom
And hoarded it from all the world:
A treasure cursed with death to those who horde it,
Given to pay for injustices done.

Regin forged the sword for Sigurð's hand:
Gram, whose name is wrath, of much renown.
Sigurðr lay in wait in the serpent's path
And thrust his sword into the beast.

His arm was bloody to the shoulder:
He told the beast his name and family.
As Fafnir died, Sigurð rode forth
To claim the treasure as his own.

To all who horde the wealth of others,
To all who keep their riches to themselves,
To all who seek to guard their knowledge
And never let their joy disperse:
We know your names and know your face.
We hear your voices in our ears.
We will not let them be our own.

We share our wealth with each other,
Bound together in frith as kin.
We join our voices and call to Kindreds
And even share our wealth with you.

Take this drink and set aside
The anger and the selfishness,
For if you join our rite this day,
Accepting this drink from our own hands,
You stand with us, as kin.

Redhead Hottie Invocation

By Rev. Michael J Dangler

Eris, Baby, Redhead Hottie,
Drinkin' chai and sippin' latte:
Take your children back to Night
And dance until the morning light.

Process from here, or maybe loiter
Or party here outside the border.
Drink and dance and have some fun
And argue who's the Prettiest One.

Outdwellers Offering

By Tanrinia

You who stood against gods and men
Titan, Jotuns, Fomhoire
Ancient and mighty

Spirits of this land who have been disturbed by our presence

Restless dead who wander

All those spirits whose purposes are not allied with ours
We ask you to let us pass, and trouble not our workings
And we shall not trouble yours

We offer this [ale] as a sign of our truce.

Misc. Ritual Notes

Spirit's Prayer
By Irisa

Daily I thank thee for the elemental garden that is life.

Earth,
the eternal mother who embodies, loves and nurtures, through all life stages, be you plant or animal.

Air,
whose gentle breezes bring forth the seeds of inspiration and the strength of communication.

Fire,
The Eternal Father whose light and love warms Mother Earth, bringing forth bud and bloom.

Water,
Whose tides guide the ebb and flow of emotions and whose gentle rains carry Spirit's life force to all creation.

Spirit,
The guiding force that is the spark of love and light, hope and beauty, life and death with all; past, present and future.

May I never forget the gift that binds all creation,
The Elemental Garden

A Prayer for After a Rite
By Anna Banana

What we have done here is good.
We have kept good company.
We have done good works.
Now we bring this goodness out into the world.
Let us seek good company.
Let us do good works.

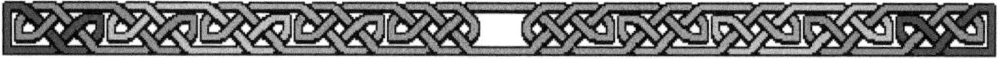

MJD & Meghan at the Temple of Poseidon

Rituals for Self-Blessing and Devotion

These rituals are designed to be as simple as possible for the first-time ritualist, but powerful enough that even an experienced liturgist could find deep meaning in daily use.

Pre-Devotional Prayer

By Irisa

[Light prayer/devotional candle]

> *May the brightness of this flame*
> *reflect the sincerity of my words*

[Light incense]

> *may the smoke carry my words to the four winds*
> *may the four winds carry my words to the realms*
> *may the Shining Ones, Ancestors, kindred and Nature Spirits hear my prayers*

A Simple Self Blessing

By Rev. Michael J Dangler

Stand before your altar. Relax, and begin.

Feel the earth below you, the firm ground. Experience the earth as upholding you, as maintaining your weight. Feel the earth holding you, rather than you pushing against the earth.

> *Earth Mother, I stand upon you today and recognize that we begin with you and we will end with you. Uphold me now as I give praise, and support me as I receive blessing.*
>
> *A child of the earth, I come before the Gods, the Spirits of Nature, and the Ancestors to offer praise. I seek to establish ties, to offer to them and open to them in return.*
>
> *The waters support and surround me.*
> *The land extends about me.*
> *The sky stretches out above me.*

At the center burns a living flame.[6]

I call out to the Keeper of the Gates.
Though I walk on uncertain paths,
Though I travel on unmapped ground,
Guide me, ward me, and relay my voice
As I offer prayers and praise.

In your mind's eye, see the sacred center open before you: watch the mists part, see the door to the Otherworld open, or watch the spiral of the magic from between the worlds reveal the Otherworld. The Gates are now open, and the true work can begin.

I call out to my ancestors, those who came before me, you of my blood and you of my heart. I seek to give you praise, to remember you now, and to honor you.

Think on your ancestors: see their faces, smile with joy at their presence. If you have praise to give them, do so now.

I call out to the spirits of this place, the spirits of nature who are the soul of this land. I seek to give you praise, to call out to you now, and to honor you.

Think on the nature spirits: the faeries of the wood, the spirits of the land. If you have praise to give them, do so now.

I call out to the deities, first children, eldest and wisest. It is you to whom we look for guidance, and you who grant the greatest blessings. I seek to give you praise, to honor you now, to give you due worship.

Think on the deities: the great ones who bless our lives, who watch over us and show us that unconditional love. If you have praise to give them, do so now.

[optional] - If you have a patron deity, one that you might wish to offer to specifically, now is the time to do that. If not, simply move to the next portion.

Today, I have given of my praise and myself.
With love in my heart and devotion on my tongue
I call out now, with all my soul:
Accept my praises!

---

[6] Serith, 36. As you speak these words, visualize the world as described here: the waters support the land, and the sky stretches out above us. This living flame burns at the center, and at the center of each of us.

Take a moment to visualize, as you shout this last statement, all of your blessings, praise, and intent flowing up to the gods, out to the spirits of nature, and down to the ancestors. Hold yourself in that moment, watching your praises flow from you, and prepare yourself for what may be offered in return.

Now, take your divination tool up.

As I have given praise to the Powers, I open to them. If there are blessings to be had, what might the nature of those blessings be?

Draw three symbols: one for the Ancestors, one for the Nature Spirits, and one for the Deities. Examine each one, think about the omen offered, and consider how it might translate into blessings.

Now, take these omens and concentrate on them, holding forth a cup of water or other beverage, saying:

Indeed, the Powers offer me blessings. Now I seek the manifestation of those blessings, the outpouring from the Powers that offer them. To those who enter this exchange, pour forth your blessings into my cup!

Envision the blessings before you, either as a mist, or a vortex of energy, or as pictographic representations of individual blessings. Watch them pour into the cup, mixing and infusing with the liquid already inside.

This in my hands is a holy cup of magic, the great blessings offered to me as joyful return of my praises to the Kindreds. Here are the deep waters that flow within the earth and that rain from the sky. These are the waters of life!

I accept this blessing, and I drink it with love and knowledge of the Powers!

(drink)

Now, with joy in my heart, I give thanks: To the Deities, thank you for your blessings. To the Nature Spirits, thank you for your blessings. To the Ancestors, thank you for your blessings. To all those Powers who have aided me, thank you for your blessings.

[If you made an offering to a patron above, make sure you thank him or her first: thank in the reverse order from invitation.]

To the Keeper of the Gates
For guiding me and warding me
Thank you for your protection.

In your mind's eye, see the sacred center close before you: watch the mists gather, see the door to the Otherworld close, or watch the spiral of the magic from between the worlds close in on the Otherworld. The Gates are now closed, and this rite is ending.

Mother of all, to you I will return all things I have left unused. For supporting and upholding me in this rite, I thank you!
This rite is ended!

You should take all your unused offerings and empty them out, and remember that cleaning the altar and space is as important as setting it up.

Daily Devotonal
By Seamus

All Hail the mother Earth.
Thank you for all your blessings.
You who cradles me in your arms, who feeds me, clothes me and keeps me.
I thank you, I ask that you walk with me today and help me to remember you and to walk softly and leave only footprints. (Offering given)

Hail to my Ancestors.
You who have become before me.
You of blood and spirit, mind and body.
You who have taught me lessons of love and honor.
I thank you. (Offering given)

Hail to the Land Spirits
My brother and sisters,
Of rock and stone, tree and twig,
My totem guides, and you of fur, feather, scale and skin
You who remind me that I am but one in the world: not above or below but beside, in the circle…
I thank you. (Offering given)

Hail to the Shining Ones
To Tyr and Thor, To Brigit and Angus
My Matron and Patrons.
You who shine down your love and blessings!
I thank you. (Offering given)

To the mighty, noble kindred; I thank you for all your blessings. For the blessings of health and happiness, enough wealth to survive, for protecting my friends and family I thank you. My I walk in honor, balance, and service

Devotional Prayer

By Maggie Collins

Gods, guide me, love me, protect me.
Take from me those weaknesses that you will
and grant me the strength to bear those that you won't.
Teach me to know and honor you.
Nature Spirits, Ancestors, surround me, support me.
Kindred , impart on me your wisdom.
My heart is open, willing and desperately wanting for you to go with my every step.

Daily House Blessing

By Shawneen

This blessing is said standing on the stairs in my house at a small shrine located there. A portion of my daily devotionals said just before leaving for the day.

All Mother, First Father
Standing between the worlds,
Your child calls to you and asks that you bless us. . .
Our home and our household
Our family, friends, and fur-kin.
From found to beam. . .
Thresholds, hearth, and rooftree.
From the mark stones of our holding
To the center of our nemeton.
Keep us from disorder. . .
Protect us. . .
Help us to know peace!
Bio Se'ailadh

Morning Lararium Prayer

By Rev. Jenni Hunt

    The Paterfamilias was traditionally responsible for leading the household each morning in a prayer to the deities of the household (the Lar and Penates) to thank them for keeping watch over the welfare and prosperity of the home and household and to ask that the coming day be fruitful and safe. In ancient times, the Paterfamilias was the male head of the household; however in modern times, this need not be so. Just as the Paterfamilias of the community is responsible for the spiritual welfare of the community, the Paterfamilias of the household is responsible for maintaining a proper relationship between the deities and the household.

    This particular prayer is designed to be performed before the lararium early in the morning after the Paterfamilias has been cleaned and purified, but before breakfast. The Paterfamilias stands before the lararium with arms outstretched and greets the household spirits:

    Salve Lar Familiaris!
       Greetings, household Lar!
    Salvete Di Penates!
       Greetings, Divine Penates!
    {If you are making an offering, do so while speaking these lines; otherwise, omit the passages in brackets.}
    Vos precor {hoc sacrificio obmovendo bonas preces} uti sitis volentes
    propitii mihi, {liberisque mei,} domo meo, familiaeque meae.
       I humbly ask that you may bestow your blessing upon me, {my children,} my home, and my household.
    {Mactete hoc sacrificio}
       {Be thou increased by this which I give to you.}
    Ita est!
       So be it!

    This is a great time for a few moments of daily meditation, particularly giving thought to what your plans, expectations, and hopes for the day may be and how the kindred spirits may be included and helpful during the day. A daily offering is not necessary, but is always an option, particularly if you seek especial favor that day. Moreover, this would be an ideal time for making a prepared or extemporaneous prayer or vow to a deity (or deities) for assistance in a particular situation. For example, when I had to leave my car at the shop for the day, I prayed to and made a vow to Mercurius (as one who is associated with commerce and fair business deals), Vulcanus (as one who is associated with metalwork and the forge fire), and any other deity who may have been able to assist me in keeping the cost of the repairs to a minimum. (It seemed to work, by the way; I had a loose spark plug which was easily reconnected and my mechanic didn't charge me a dime!)

Grove Devotional

By Rev. Michael J Dangler

At ComFest in 2006 and again in 2007, Three Cranes Grove, ADF, did short devotional rituals every three hours for three days. They were hectic, but they were very, very good for us.

In light of ComFest being a recurring theme with the Grove, we wanted to provide this, and explain a bit about it.

First, have each person find their center, then speak:

We stand at the Center
In the presence of All
Our feet supported by the Earth Mother
Our minds crowned in Inspiration
Our hearts pure of purpose.

[devotional prayers/offerings/etc.]

Our hearts remain open,
Our minds retain their fire,
Our feet are still supported,
As we depart this place.
May we take our center with us.
This rite is ended.

The central hope was that we could find a way to do our usual opening prayers without going too deeply in depth. So, we took our normal order of opening prayers, and basically:

1. Asked folks to find their center,
2. noted our usual descriptive cosmos prayer,
3. acknowledged the Earth Mother,
4. called on inspiration,
5. and reminded us to think on the purpose.

Then we did a short devotional prayer or offering to the Kindred/Power/entity that we were doing the devotional for.

After that, we simply returned ourselves by doing it backwards.

It worked quite well for us, and we really like this very simple, very easy form of devotional.

Kindred Devotional Prayer

by Seamus

Ancestors walk with me today and always,
Thank you for your lessons and sacrifices.
To the well I give offerings and ask my ancestors
Those of blood and bone, those of spirit and faith,
Those who have blazed the trails before me so that I may walk easier,
I praise and thank you.
Hail the Ancestors.

Nature Spirits walk with me today and always,
Thank you for your lessons and sacrifices.
To the tree I give offerings and ask my Nature Spirits
Those of stone and soil, tree and leaf, blood and bone,
Those who dance the spiral dance with me so that I may walk in balance,
I praise and thank you.
Hail the Nature Spirits

Shining Ones walk with me today and always,
Thank you for your wisdom and blessings.
To the fire I give offerings and ask my Shining Ones
Those of my grove, those of my hearth, and those of my heart.
You who light the way with your brilliance, may I walk in virtues.
I praise and thank you.
Hail the Shining Ones

A Silent Solitary Rite:

By Rev. Michael J Dangler

This rite is done in silence, though words can be used with it. It is a full ADF-style ritual written to be as simple as possible, for any need you might have.

I) Approach your altar, either before bed, after waking, or when you feel you need it.

II) Fill the Well and light three candles, which are your triple Flame. Touch your representation of the tree.

III) Breathe in deeply nine times.

IV) Open the Gates:
- A) Call on Garanus to join his Magic with yours, silently or verbally.
- B) Open each gate: the Well, the Fire, and the Tree, respectively. See the Gates open as you do this.
- C) Either simply open yourself to the Powers, or make offering, depending on what you feel is right.
- D) Call upon your ancestors, the nature spirits, and the deities, silently. Speak from the heart.
- E) Call upon your Patron, if you have one. You might also call out to see if a Patron wishes to present him/herself.
- F) Meditate or open yourself to the words of the Gods and Goddesses. Usually, these are very, very private words.
- G) Thank the Powers for coming, and ask that they go in peace.

V) Close the Gates.
- A) Again, ask Garanus to join his Magic with yours.
- B) Close each Gate: Tree, Fire, and Well, respectively.
- C) Thank Garanus for his presence, and ask that He go in peace.

VI) Extinguish the candles and either go to bed or go on with your day.

A Prayer for Establishing a Frith-stead

This is a prayer or invocation to set a frith-stead at a festival.

Frith-stead Prayer

By Seamus

Hail Tyr! Great Sky father, Guardian of Order, God of the Thing we call on you tonight and ask that you hallow this land for our gathering. May our hearts be true, may our cause be just, and may we act with honor and frith.

Warrior's Pronouncement

By Seamus

I stand here today not as a Bard, though I speak from the heart.
Not as a historian, though I have learned my lessons well.
Not as Seer, though I keep a watchful eye.
Not a clergy, though I offer up my council,
I stand not as a leader, brewer, dancer or healer;
do not judge me for what I am, but for what you are.
Without me, you could exist in the comfort that life affords you.
I am the beacon in the night, the fire against the cold.
I am what binds the wolf of chaos and sets things right.
I sacrifice myself for the good of the tribe. I am a Warrior!

The Invocation of the Four Winds

By Rev. Jenni Hunt

From the east, I draw the breath of Eurus;
its rosy glow piercing the darkest of nights.
I exhale its winged morning song into this grove.
From the south, I draw the breath of Auster,
its moist warmth permitting a time of leisure.
I exhale its steamy summer brew into this grove.
From the west, I draw the breath of Zephyrus,
its western shore lit with the fires of inspiration.
I exhale its dusky shimmering sensuality into this grove.
From the north, I draw the breath of Boreas,
its roaring wind sending us home to the warmth of our hearths.
I exhale its icy-tongued blast into this grove.
In this grove, we share all these and each other's breath;
breathing as one at the center.

A Two Powers Attunement

By Rev. Jenni Hunt

Take a moment to find the center of your mind, body and soul.

Breathe deeply from your belly the air in this sacred grove, charged with anticipation and potential. Exhale fully through your mouth; then, through your nose, fill your lungs with the clean, cool aroma of this moment. Allow that sacred air to circulate and surge throughout your body.

Now continuing to breathe from your belly, stand firm and feel the Earth's pulse through the soles of your feet. Curl your toes into the ground, rooting yourself into the bosom of the warm, nurturing Earth, Draw another deep breath while imagining tendrils of roots and vines connecting yourself with the soil beneath you.

Now stretch forth your hands to those closest to you, and grasp hands or simply touch them, if you can. At one with the cosmos and at one as a grove - we are, as a community, greater than the sum of our parts. We stand as a grove in a forest of trees, one folk.

The waters support and surround us
The land extends about us
The sky stretches out above us.
At our center burns a living flame.
May all the Kindred bless us.
May our worship be true.
May our actions be just.
May our love be pure.
Blessings, and honor, and worship to the Holy Ones.

Seamus' DP Oath

Grandfathers, grandfathers, your son calls out to you, may I honor you and our family with my words and deeds. I am grateful for the lessons you have taught me, in your arms I learned about honor and right action.

Grandmothers, grandmothers, your son calls out to you, may I honor you and our family with my words and deeds. I am grateful for the lessons you have taught me, in your arms I learned about love and kindness.

Hail and welcome to my animal guides, the blue heron and the mighty buck. Thank you for your lessons. May I draw upon your wisdom and strength. May I always remember that I am but a child of our mother and that my place is within the circle.

Hail Tyr! Great Sky father, Guardian of Order, God of the Thing. First to call to me so long ago even before I knew you, you who walks with me, teaches me, and reminds me to be true to my heart, and to act with honor and frith. I hail and honor you.

Hail Angus MacOg! You who I first called to, you show me love and the sacrifice that must accompany it. You who walks with me and reminds me of beauty of the world. I hail and honor you.

Hail Thor! Red Beard, Odin's son. Worm's bane. You who walks with me and teaches me to walk in courage, to be ready to face the world, to enjoy life and those you share it with. I hail and honor you.

Hail to Brigit! My Goddess of inspiration. You who walks with me and teaches me to be creative and to continue to grow and learn. I hail and honor you.

115

To my ancestors, nature allies and deities, I stand here today to proclaim myself to walk with you. To learn from you and if our paths should part to remember the lessons you have taught me.

Devotional

By Anna Gail

I oath that today I stand here as a dedicant along the path of ADF. I oath to be true to myself and to be a steward to the grove and ADF community for as long as it resonates in my heart.

Mighty Norns, Urd, Verdandi, Skud
Ladies of fate, Thurs-maids
Weavers, carvers, counselors, nourishers
Deliverers of Destiny to god and man alike
Guard well my wyrd that I may walk a steady path
Carve wisdom, peace, honor and joy deep into my orlog
I give you hail for all you do for the nine realms, Hail the Norns!

Hela, daughter of Lopt
Guarder of Graves
Warder and care-giver for the dead of all the realms
Walker of two-worlds
I honor you this day
Walk beside me that I will be a cause for pride for those that came before
For the lessons and wisdom you bring I give you Thanks and Hail.

Vidar, silent-As
Son of Odin, Shoe-wearer
Counselor for the All-father
Avenger, Huntsman, Woodsman
I honor you this day
Walk with me that I show wisdom in all my counsel and bring honor to my path
Warrior, I give you hail and thanks!

Mighty Kindreds: Shining Ones, Ancestors, Land-vettir
I give you hail and thanks for the parts you play in my path
Allow me to walk softly but firmly that I will be a joy to those around me
Let there be peace in my heart, love in my touch, wisdom in my words and hospitality from my hearth.
Hail the Kindreds!

Take an Omen for the day and see what you should pay attention to and work on.

Daily Devotional

By Tanrinia

This is done in the morning and the evening. It is designed to maintain relationships with spirit guides, kindred, and a single pantheon of deities, rather than just focusing on a patron deity.

1. Nine breaths meditation, to ground and center.

2. Establishing the three realms:

> *The Sky extends above me*
> *The Land stretches about me*
> *The Sea surrounds and supports me.*

3. Establishing the gates (taken from various ADF Norse liturgies)

(Light the candle)

> *I kindle the sacred fire, in wisdom, love, and power*
> *Sacred fire burn within me*

(Pour water into bowl for well)

> *From the depths flow the waters of wisdom*
> *Sacred well flow within me*

(Acknowledge the tree symbol)

> *From the depths to the heights spans the world tree*
> *Sacred tree grow within me*
>
> *The Fire, the Well, the Sacred Tree*
> *Flame and flow and grow in me*
> *Thus my sacred grove is claimed and hallowed.*
> *By the cleansing of the Fire and the Water let all ill turn from me and mine.*
> *So Be It.*

4. Earth Mother

(touch stone on altar that represents Earth mother)

Earth mother, source of all life, final destination.
I give thanks for the night [day]
And ask your blessings, protection, and wisdom for the day [night]

5. Open the gates/spirit guide

(While speaking this, I draw the druid's sigil vertically in the air above the altar. When I ask for the gates to be opened, I take my hands and visualize physically parting the veil between the worlds as if it were a curtain.)

Owl above me (hand at top of circle)
Bear beside me (hand travels clockwise around)
Snake below me (hand at bottom of circle)
Join your magic with mine (complete circle)
As we walk the elder ways together (draw the two lines of the sigil)
Let the gates be open. (Part the veil starting where the two lines of the sigil are, and pushing to the side, as if opening curtains.)

6. 3 Kindreds

(I have a three-bowl container on the altar that receives the offerings for each of the kindred. I try to use the cultural language for each of the kindred when possible. The below is written for Norse. Invocations can be lengthier also, depending upon time available.)

Landvaettir who allow me to share their domain.
Housevaettir who protect and ward my home.
I give thanks for the night [day] (put lavender petals in bowl)
And ask your blessings, protection, and wisdom for the day [night].

Alfar, Disir, Ancestors mine
Bones who are my bones
Whose blood runs through my veins
Whose breath is on the air that I breathe
I give thanks for the night [day] (offering of tobacco)
And ask your blessings, protection, and wisdom for the day [night]

Aesir, Vanir
Shining ones and all allied with them.
First children of the Mother
Bringers of civilization and order
I give thanks for the night [day] (offering of rose petals)

And ask your blessings, protection, and wisdom for the day [night].

7. Deity du jour

(Changes depending upon the day. This is up to the particular individual and their pantheon. The invocation would change daily, but it all ends with...}

> *I give thanks for the night [day]* (light appropriate incense)
> *And ask your blessing, protection, and wisdom for the day [night].*

8. Omen

(When asking for blessings, protection, and wisdom, I pull a rune or ogham.)

9. Prayers

(as needed)

10. Thanks

> *(Deity of the day), I thank you*
> *Shining ones, Mighty ones, Noble ones, I thank you.*
>
> *May my words be true*
> *May my actions be just*
> *May my thoughts be clear*
> *And may my heart be pure*
> *That I may bring honor to my Kindreds, my family, and myself.*
> *So be it.*

11. Close gates

(I basically repeat the druid sigil as above. Again, substitute your own spirit guides.)

> *Owl above me*
> *Bear beside me*
> *Snake below me*
> *Join your magic with mine once more*
> *As we walk into the day [night] together*
> *Let the gates be closed!* (reverse the hand symbol, pulling the veil or curtain between the worlds closed.)

Spirit guides, I thank you.

12. Earth mother

Earth mother I thank you.

(Extinguish candle, pour water from bowl, back into container.)

Daily Prayers
By Nick Egilhoff

Morning Prayer
Said upon rising in the morning.

Blessed Kindreds,
Thank you for restful sleep and interesting dreams,
And may today be a good day.
Hail and thank you.

Morning Prayer to Sunna
Said at dawn or whenever you first see the sun in the morning (prior to noon).

Hail Sunna, you of the golden face and hair whose countenance warms and enlivens us
all.
As you saddle Skinfaxi and prepare for the day's ride,
May you be swift and mighty,
May you evade the jaws of the hungry wolf,
May your radiance guide us toward virtue throughout the day.
Hail Sunna!

Noon Prayer to Sunna
Said as close to noon as possible.

Hail to Sunna:
The shining golden light of the heavens!
As you reach the zenith of your day's journey,
May your might and main shine forth from the roof of the world,
Serving as a beacon for our hearts, our minds, and our spirits.
Hail Sunna!

Evening Prayer to Sunna

Said at sunset.

Blessed Sunna, as you seek the comfort of the horizon
May you rest your weary body,
May you relax contentedly in the dark cloak of the night,
And may you rise once again with the morning.

Evening Prayer to Mani

Said at any point during the night, especially when the moon is visible.

Blessed Mani, you of shifting guises,
May your might and main protect us,
May your silvery light guide us:
No matter how dark the night,
No matter how close the wolf,
No matter how hidden your face might be.
Blessed Mani, watch over us.

Evening Prayer

Said at night before going to sleep.

I give thanks to the Blessed Kindreds,
For all their blessings and their boons,
For the gifts and the wisdom they have given me this day
Whether I am aware of them or not.
Hail and thank you.

Meal Prayer

Said (obviously) before eating.

Mighty Thor, bless and hallow this meal
As I give thanks to the wights who gave of themselves so that I might eat this day.
Hail, and thank you all.

Nature Awareness Meditation

As Druids, we should always be seeking ways to connect to nature. This is a simple meditation to help you connect to the natural world around you.

Begin by simply breathing in the air that is around you. Consider that this air is not man-made, but is part of the cycles of life all around you. The oxygen that we breathe is the by-product of photosynthesis, and the carbon dioxide you exhale is a by-product we create that the plants need to survive. Already we are connected to nature.

With your eyes closed, try to separate the scents in the air. Can you smell the rain? Does the smell of mulch around the trees lining your street reach you? Find the scents carried on the wind, and categorize them.

Place your hands on the ground. Feel the earth through the palms of your hands, or if you're inside, feel the texture of the carpet or floor beneath you. Consider what caused the ground to feel as it does, and try to make out different things that make it up.

Can you taste the air? What tastes can you discern? If you're sitting in the rain or snow, open your mouth and catch a drop or flake. Taste it.

Listen to the world around you. Pick out sounds and isolate them, so you hear only them. Open your mind to them, and concentrate for a while. Is it a natural sound, such as a bird chirping, or is it a man made sound, such as a freeway. Consider how these things fit into nature to make a complete picture.

Open your eyes and look about you. If you're inside, try to spot nature and how it has invaded "civilized" domains. If you're outside, concentrate on something small and natural, focus on something. It could be a small section of tree bark, or a single small animal. Watch it for a time, studying it. Now, pull back your focus and look at the whole world, adding one sense at a time, and feel the connection you have to the earth.

Prayer for the end of the day
By Rev. Michael J Dangler

Long ago the sun has set
and the last rays of day have faded.
Ratri comes across the sky,
reliable as her sister each morning.

Night is not the darkness,
nor the things feared by all:
Ratri is the lady of shining stars,
of moonlight reflecting on the waters.
Draw forth the treasures,
uncover them and cast wide their covering.
Ratri draws the riches of night
into the open for those who honor her.

So as the sky darkens,
shine your light upon me.
Ratri, I offer to you,
who keeps us safe from harm.

Prayer Bead Devotional

By Mary Anne

Shortly after joining ADF and becoming a friend to Three Cranes Grove, I started seriously working on my Dedicant Path materials. I had been trying to get through my Nine virtues articles and was finding I was having a lot of trouble motivating myself to do them. I had been browsing the articles on ADF's website and stumbled across one by Susan Reed called "An ADF Nine Virtues Bead Devotional." The idea intrigued me so I read on. After reading the entire article several times I realized that this could be something that might really help me figure out what I want to talk about in my virtues essays so I set about to create my own set of prayer beads. I borrowed heavily in some places from Susan's original devotional but in other places I felt my interpretation was much different and warranted coming up with a brand new words and ideas. It took me a couple of hours to complete the whole devotiona,l and it is still a work in progress, but it is something that I am very proud of and think on almost every day. I have yet to complete all my DP virtue articles, but the longer I meditate daily on the virtues the deeper understanding I gain from them, and I have confidence that when I finally sit down and write it all out, my daily devotional will provide me insights I would not have had otherwise.

- **First Bead** – Ancient Ones, Noble Ones, Shining Ones, I welcome you in heart and hearth. On this day may I live in such a way that I may honor you in word and action. (The bead I used for this I felt represented all three Kindreds, silver for the shining ones, antique looking for the ancestors, and floral designs for the nature spirits.)
- **Wisdom** – On this day may I have the knowledge and insight to judge appropriately. *(This bead is represented by a pearl for "pearls of wisdom")*
- **Piety** – On this day may I never forget my relationship with you and may I honor you with a joyful heart. *(I associate piety with love and devotion so it made sense that this bead was heart shaped.)*
- **Vision** – On this day may I assume nothing and open my eyes to the wider world around me. *(I chose this bead because of it being clear, you can almost see through it.)*
- **Loki** – Master of Mischief and Bringer of Change... *(Because Loki is one of my patrons I felt it only appropriate that his bead is slightly larger than the rest. I*

also tried to find the most unique bead in my collection because Loki tends to march to the beat of his own drum.)

- **Courage** – On this day may I follow the way of truth with strength and determination in spite of my fears. *(I chose red for this bead because it is often associated with bravery.)*

- **Integrity** – On this day may I remain true to my values and approach others' beliefs with tolerance and respect. *(I chose a rainbow for this bead because all of the colors exist together harmoniously.)*

- **Perseverance** – On this day may I wholeheartedly pursue my goals even in times of strife. *(I chose an orange bead because it reminded me of the sun and how it never fails to rise and fall every day.)*

- **Danu** – Queen of Kindness and Great Earth Mother... *(I chose a large brown bead for its obvious earth connections.)*

- **Hospitality** – On this day may I give to you and others with humor and grace so that I may receive in turn. *(I chose a golden bead because it reminded me of warmth and compassion.)*

- **Moderation** – On this day may I find balance in all aspects of life. *(I chose this bead because of the light and dark colors together.)*

- **Fertility** – On this day may I remember to appreciate and nurture creativity in all my endeavors. *(I chose green because I have always found green an inspirational color.)*

- **Last Bead** – Blessed Patrons and Kindred, I thank you for your gifts and wisdom and on this day may I continue to receive your challenges and blessings.

Prayer upon extinguishing candles at the end of a devotional
By Anna Banana

Even as I extinguish these flames,
I keep them burning within myself.

The altar of my heart is always open to you.

Wellspring 2008
Cranes in the Nemeton

LtoR: Seamus, lees, Shawneen, MJD, Stephanie, Mariel, Anne-with-the-Band

Core Mythology

The following meditations and rituals are designed to introduce you to the core mythology of Three Cranes Grove, ADF. The most important thing is our Inception Statement, which you will often read if you are a member of Three Cranes. In the first meditation, *The Garanus Meditation*, you will be introduced to Garanus, the Crane. He is the most common gatekeeper in Three Cranes rituals. Other information follows along and builds on these two things.

The Inception Statement

A core part of our shared mythology is the Grove Inception Statement. Spoken first on September 22, 2002, this has always been the driving statement about where our Grove is going, and where it has been. More importantly, it tells us how we have always prayed the Grove would get to where it was going.

Three Cranes Grove, ADF
Inception Statement

We have come together today for the inception of Three Cranes Protogrove, ADF, and to join together in worshiping and praising the Shining Ones.

A Protogrove needs to be nurtured as it grows. It needs an influx of new ideas, a creative flow that will soak its roots and keep it strong and firm. It needs leadership to show it the heights it may attain, and dedicated gardeners to tend it and guide it to its destination. It needs the sunlight of enlightened minds to warm it and to synthesize energy and vigor. It needs faith in the Gods and Goddesses to grow straight and true.

If the flow of ideas grows stagnant, or the leadership and sunlight fail, the trees will not grow, but will wither and die. Without faith in the Gods and Goddesses, our work is in vain, for it is Their hands which guide our work. This Grove is our responsibility, for we have planted it.

We must not fail it, for it will never fail us.

The Garanus Meditation

When Three Cranes Grove, ADF, started doing public ritual, we chose not to call on a deity for a gatekeeper, though there were many available. We wanted to build a relationship with a nature spirit, helping to spread our worship across the Kindred. We spent some time working with various nature spirits, and as I look back on it I'm a bit surprised how long it took us to see the perfect nature spirit: we needed to look no further than our name.

For two full years, we invoked the crane, named Garanus after the Gaulish word for "crane." In September 2005, we added a new piece to the invocation: a meditation that precedes the actual invocation.

The meditation is a method I learned at the Trillium Gathering in 2005, when ADF's Vice Archdruid Kirk Thomas gave a workshop on "Circles of Concentration in Ritual." The meditation helps the ritual participants to focus on the opening of the gates, and helps put them into a frame of mind where the energy raising of the gate opening is more accessible.

This meditation is done just before the invocation of the Gatekeeper, and gives a set of visual cues that help to keep everyone on the same page.

This particular meditation is designed simply to re-center the Grove on the Gates of the ritual, re-establish the cosmos, and confirm each participant's frame of reference. It slows the rite down in preparation for opening the Gates.

The Garanus Meditation

In your mind's eye, see the mists that hover between the worlds as they roll in around this sacred space. In all directions, the mists close you off from the mundane world, leaving nothing but this Grove.

At the edge of the mists, there is a parting. The mists roll back to reveal the waters, deep and undisturbed. They stretch far into the distance, disappearing into the farthest mists.

In the shallows before you, where the land meets the waters, stands a tall, watchful crane. One foot stands upon the land, and the other is in the water. His eye is raised to the sky.

This is Garanus, the crane.

He has dominion over the three realms: he walks upon the land, feeds in the waters, flies through the sky, and travels beyond the sea, beyond the Ninth Wave. Garanus, the crane, will guide us and protect us as we walk to meet the Kindred at the boundaries of this sacred Grove.

The Ancestor Box Devotional

The Ancestor Box is part of our ritual gear that travels separately from our usual Grove ritual gear. This tradition began at Samhain 2004, where we began to bring items that reminded us of our ancestors and place them in the box. The box is *never* opened, until the Druid Moon before Samhain, and it is closed at the Druid Moon after Samhain. Any item that enters the box at Samhain becomes part of the Grove's ancestor worship.

The Ancestor Box changes hands at each ritual: the person who is in charge of the next ritual takes the Ancestor Box back to their home. There, it is given a place of honor in their home, and kept separate from the mundane items in the house, and brought to the next ritual by the person leading the rite. This allows the person in charge of the rite to be in perpetual contact with the Grove's shared community and ancestry.

When the box is taken home, it is the duty of its keeper to do (at least) weekly devotionals with the box. The following script can be used for these devotionals.

An Ancestor Box Prayer

By Rev. Michael J Dangler
(to be said with hands laid upon the box)

This box holds mementos,
remembrances of those gone before.
It is a treasury of remnants,
of things left behind.

The memories of the Grove's Ancestors
are tied to these things.
The Ancestors of Three Cranes
are embodied here.

As the Grove honors the Dead,
as we honor each others' Kin,
we honor our own shared Ancestry,
and welcome the Ancestors of our chosen Kin
into our own hearts and lives.
Blessings on the Ancestors of Three Cranes.

3CG Druid Moon Names

The Grove does Druid Moon Rites on the sixth night of every moon. The names of the moons are based off the Coligny Calendar, and our translations owe much to Chris Gwinn, Alexi Kondratiev, and Ariotanos.

The rituals generally follow in theme from the translation, and we encourage input on what we do and how we do it. Each of these rituals is done on the sixth night after the new moon, regardless of whether it is a week day or week end.

We also schedule the Grove's mistletoe rite for a weekend Druid Moon Rite at least twice per year. Mistletoe rites are done in place of the Druid Moon Rite for that month, and they are welcoming rites for our new Grove members. Each member is given a token that shows their membership when they go through a Mistletoe rite, and these tokens are special to our members. No one outside the Grove knows what they look like.

Month Names and Translations

Month	Gaulish	Translation
Nov.	Samonios	End of Summer month
Dec.	Dumannios	Dark month
Jan.	Rivros	Frost month
Feb.	Anagantios	Stay-at-Home month
Mar.	Ogronios	End of the Cold month
Apr.	Cutios	Rain month
May	Gaimonios	End of Winter month
Jun.	Simivisonnos	Mid-Summer month
Jul.	Equos	Horse month
Aug.	Elembivios	Many-Sided month
Sep.	Ædrinios	End of Heat month
Oct.	Cantlos	Song month
Inter-Calary	Antaranos	In-Between month

Three Fires Devotional Meditation

During Summerset 2005, the Grove was given the opportunity to do the main ritual for the festival. When we asked what the ritual should be about, we were told, "Oh, it's a ritual to light the bonfire." This left us scratching our heads, as "to light a bonfire" is not the kind of intent our Grove works with.

As we discussed the ritual, we decided to bless the fire by lighting it from three fires that we had made sacrifice to: the Fire of Blessings (more correctly termed the Fire of Sacrifice), the Fire of Fellowship, and the Fire of Inspiration. From these three fires, we lit the central fire, the Fire of Unity. This ritual built one of the strongest bonds between Grove members that we have ever forged, and it is the turning point in our Grove that lead us from being a group of people who do ritual, and transformed us into "one light, one depth, one united and sacred Grove."

This meditation is designed to draw that back in to our hearts. For this rite, you will need three candles (or three fires, if it's possible) that are unlit, and a box of matches.

The Three Fires

Within me is a well of deep potential, of great creativity. This well is shining with an inner light, as a fire in the waters. This fire shapes and transforms the potential into action.

[Strike a match. Light each fire as you speak its name.]

I take this fire from the waters within me, and reach out to bring this action into this realm. I light the Fire of Sacrifice before me, the Fire of Inspiration to my left, and the Fire of Fellowship to my right.
With each Fire lit, I push my will out into the world.
1. May I always remember the Kindreds
2. May I always know the answers within me
3. May I always be part of a greater community
And may each of these fires burn as one Fire of Unity within me.

[visualize the fires at three points feeding the fire within you]

This Fire of Unity binds me to the Grove: bound by the sacrifices we make, speaking with a voice that is made of many while guided by one, and always having a hearth fire to pray at.
Blessings, honor and worship to the Holy Ones.

Two Powers, Inner Gates Meditation

In our Druid Moon Rites, the folk enter a space where the Gates are already open, where the Spirits are already fully present and aware of our intentions. Because of this, we needed a new form of attunement, one that informed the gathered Folk where they were, and how the sacred center could resonate within them individually. From this, our Inner Gates meditation was formed.

The Inner Gates

You have come now to stand at the crossroads, at the boundaries of the worlds. The Gates stand open before you. In this space, we are open entirely to the Kindreds. Take a moment to connect yourself to the vertical axis of this space, and the Gates:

Before you, see the Well, reaching deep into the worlds below, into the realm of the Ancestors, into the world of the chthonic deities, into the dark, cool waters. The waters of this Well spring from deep within the bosom of the earth, drawing up these waters so that we may access them.

Within each of us, a cauldron warms our loins, a Cauldron of Potential. This Cauldron is the source of our renewal, our bounty, and our energy. See this Cauldron in your mind's eye.

Now, take a moment to join the Cauldron in your loins to the Well before you. Feel them merge and change, and feel the Gate that is open in this place open within you. Fill yourself with the powers welling from below.

Now, turn your attention to the Fire before you. Watch the flames dance and spin, reaching ever higher into the sky above, reflecting and opening to the powers of heaven, the warm, electric sky power. The Fire we have built on the bosom of the earth lifts our praises and prayers to the realm of the Holy Ones who inhabit the sky.

Within each of us, a fire burns brightly in our heads, a Fire of Inspiration, shaping and forming our thoughts into actionable states. This fire is kindled in our heads at birth, and it burns more brightly when we feed it through cultivation of wisdom and knowledge.

Take a moment now and join the Fire of Inspiration in your head with the Fire of Sacrifice before you. Feel them merge and change, and feel the Gate that is open in the fire open within you. Fill yourself with the powers of the sky.

Turn your attention now to the Tree that is before us, upholding the worlds and supporting the cosmos. Know its rough bark and its strong limbs. Know the paths that the branches take as they stretch skyward, and the places the roots delve to as they reach deep within the earth. The Tree before us is the world tree, axis and support of all the worlds.

Within you now, feel the Two Powers . . . They mix and meld, the light of the heavens shining upon the waters of the earth, reflecting like burning dawn on the sea . . . These powers form a pillar within us, recreating the cosmos from our very bodies.

Take a moment now and join the World Tree and this shining pillar of cosmic light within you. Feel them merge and change, and feel the Gate that is open in the Tree open within you. Feel the powers of earth and sky as they shine out from you.

Around you, there are many trees. There is a strong Grove. Feel your branches entwine as you reach out your hands. Each of us is supported by the land, we are crowned by the sky, and our roots drink of the cosmic waters. Together we are one united, sacred Grove: the shining fire at the center of all the worlds.

May our worship be true, may our actions be just, and may our love be pure. Blessings, honor, and worship to the Holy Ones.

Consecrating the Waters of Life

This script was worked up for the Return Flow, based off the ADF Core Order of Ritual, with stage directions. The only tools required are two pitchers (one larger, one smaller: clear glass is good for both because you can visually see the separation when it occurs, and the Grove has noticed that if they are held just right, the officiant can catch the sun or the candles in the waters) and three candles:

I: Calling for Blessing

These are indeed powerful omens;
take a moment to reflect upon them.
Consider first how these blessings affect you,
how you can find their expression in your life.

Next consider how these blessings relate to us all,
how the community as a whole, and this Grove in particular
might be affected by the Great Ones' blessings.

Now, in your mind's eye, see the blessings manifest:
A mist around us, a shining ray from the heavens,
a deep welling from the bosom of the earth.
See the blessings in your own way,
And know the Gods pour them out for you.

II: Hallowing the Waters

[elevate larger pitcher]

All waters are by nature sacred,
welling from the earth or falling from the sky,
but today, we separate these waters *
Asking that they be infused with the blessings of the Kindreds.

[* - pour the waters into a smaller vessel as you speak this line]

[At this point, set the waters in the center of three candles, unlit as yet. Source note: we picked this up from Ian Corrigan]

Ancient and mighty ones, we have honored you,
And you have offered us blessings in turn:
Shining Ones, give us the Waters!

All: Shining Ones, give us the Waters!

[First candle lit]

Your blessings mingle with the waters before us,
Infusing them, becoming one with them:
Shining Ones, give us the Waters!

All: Shining Ones, give us the Waters!

[Second candle lit]

In all the ways your blessings may come, in all their forms,
mixing with the waters here, shining and bright with your love for us:
Shining Ones, give us the Waters!

All: Shining Ones, give us the Waters!

[Third candle lit]

*[Pause for a moment, and hold your hand, wand, or sickle over the waters.
Direct the energy from the Grove into the container.]*

These Waters now hold the blessings of the Gods,
The outpouring of love from the Great Ones
As we share in these sacred waters,
we drink in wisdom, strength and blessing.

[elevate the Waters]

Behold, the Waters of Life!

All: Behold, the Waters of Life!

III: Affirming the Blessing

Children of the Earth, before you is the holy cup
Do you wish to share in these blessings?

All: We do!

Then, as the waters are poured out,
know that they hold blessings for you and this grove and this community.
Work well with these blessings, Children of the Earth.

[Waters are passed out, and quaffed]

Now we have imbibed the Waters of Life,
the outpouring of blessings from the Powers.
Feel the waters within you,
and know that we have been blessed.

Seeking the Fire of Piety: A Meditation

This is a meditation from Rev. Michael J Dangler's book, Cultivating the Fire of Piety: Druidic Piety in a Modern Age.

It is up to each of us to find the Flames of Belief and the Fuel of Action within ourselves and to bring them together. Once we have brought the fuel to the flames, the Fire of Piety is born from their synthesis.

Kneel with your back straight, resting on your heels. Let yourself be settled in place, relaxed. Let the worries of the day go: know that you are here, in this time, for magic.

Move your hands up to your chest. One hand should be cupped below your sternum, and one above it. Hold your arms out from your body, rather than relaxed to the sides. It is in the space between your hands that we will find the Fire of Piety manifesting.

Take nine deep breaths. When each breath fills your lungs, hold it in for a moment, and then let it out in a controlled, measured manner. Watch each inbreath and outbreath as they occur, noting each feeling in your body.

Turn your attention now to the space between your hands.

Over your heart, a flame burns brightly. Some may know this flame well already, and others may only now be making its acquaintance. Whatever your relationship, gaze at it now and experience the flame's luster. See the light from it, and note where in you this light is reflected within you.

These flames are the Flames of Belief.

Feel its warmth, listen to it crackle. This flame is a flame that burns and hungers for fuel, and you are the only person who can feed it.

Now, as you consider this flame, the warmth it creates, and the deep comfort you feel as it burns within you, consider how you can build it larger. Within yourself, find those things that can fuel the flames before you. You might see this as large logs, sticks of kindling, or clarified butter.

This is the Fuel of Action.

Know that this store of fuel is never-ending, that it will feed the flames for as long as you are willing to feed it. Know, too, that each prayer we make, each offering poured out, and each sacrifice taken out of our own use is one more piece of fuel given to the flames.

This knowledge is what you have come to obtain: the location of the Flames of Belief and where you can retrieve the Fuel of Action.

Take a single piece of fuel from the pile and set it among the flames. Watch as the flames hungrily devour the fuel, and how they grow brighter and illuminate more of your being.

This is the Fire of Piety. This is the synthesis of belief and action, flame and fuel. Watch the Fire of Piety as it burns, and feel how much stronger and more vibrant you feel yourself. Enjoy the warmth and comfort the fire brings.

Now, take nine breaths again, in and out, focusing on each individual breath. On your ninth breath, find yourself back in the mundane world, let your arms relax, and sit comfortably.

Trance Script, Garanus and Meeting the Ancestors

By Rev. Michael J Dangler
Begin by making offering to Garanus, the Crane

Take a moment and find your center. . . Breathe deeply, first in. . . then out. . . then in. . . then out. Continue this breathing pattern for a moment, simply watching your breath, feeling it fill you. . . and feeling it empty fom you. . . [long pause]

While still watching your breath, begin to open your mind to magic. . . see with your inner eye as the mists of magic surround you . . . colored yet grey . . . formless, yet with shapes that arise, change, and receed back into the mists. . .

Now, see the mists part, drawing back like a curtain and revealing the cosmic waters, stretching further than your eyes can see. . . You stand on the banks of these waters now . . . these cool, endless, deep waters of the earth . . . and as you look to the place where the water meets the land, you see a crane . . . tall and majestic . . . one foot on land, one foot in the waters, and his eye raised to the heavens.

This is noble Garanus, the Crane

Know that he has domain over the three realms. . . sleeping on the land . . . feeding in the waters. . . flying through the sky . . . traveling beyond the Ninth Wave . . . A creature of all realms, beholden to none.

Approach him now, slowly but with confidence. . . watch his reactions . . . feel his gaze upon you . . . know that with him, you are safe.

Ask him to show you the ways between the worlds, to take you beyond the Ninth Wave. . . Ask to see the signposts that you might know the ways again when next you pass here. . . If there is an Ancestor to whom you wish to speak, ask to speak to them.

Climb now upon his back. Settle in, and listen to the wisdom of the Crane as he takes flight and shows you the ways and the signs that mark them [long pause]

See the world beyond the Ninth Wave as it emerges from the mists of the waters . . . the Land of the Ever Young . . . the Delightful Plain. . . Know that you are heading here, and you will soon speak to your ancestors.

As the Crane lands, again with a foot in the water and a foot on the land, you remain seated on his back. . . down the beach come a troop of the Mighty Dead, with the Ancestor you sought to speak with at their head. . . As the troop comes to a stop, your Ancestor comes down the beach to water's edge.

Hear the words your Ancestor speaks to you, giving you a message that is for your ears alone. . . [very long pause]

It is now time to take your leave, for time moves differently in these realms. . . Thank your Ancestor in your own way . . . Thank the troop of the Dead . . . Whisper now your desire to return to the Crane. . . Feel him take flight back across the sea.

The return trip is faster . . . note the signs and landmarks on your way home . . .

Find yourself back at the edge of the waters, in the mists of magic you left so long ago. Thank the Crane who has taken you this far. . . Listen to any words he might say to you. . . remember the lessons.

Again, see the mists of magic roll in and surround you. . . See the formless shapes, the colored grey. . . find yourself again at your center. . . Begin to move your fingers and toes, getting comfortable back in your body. Awaken, and relax.

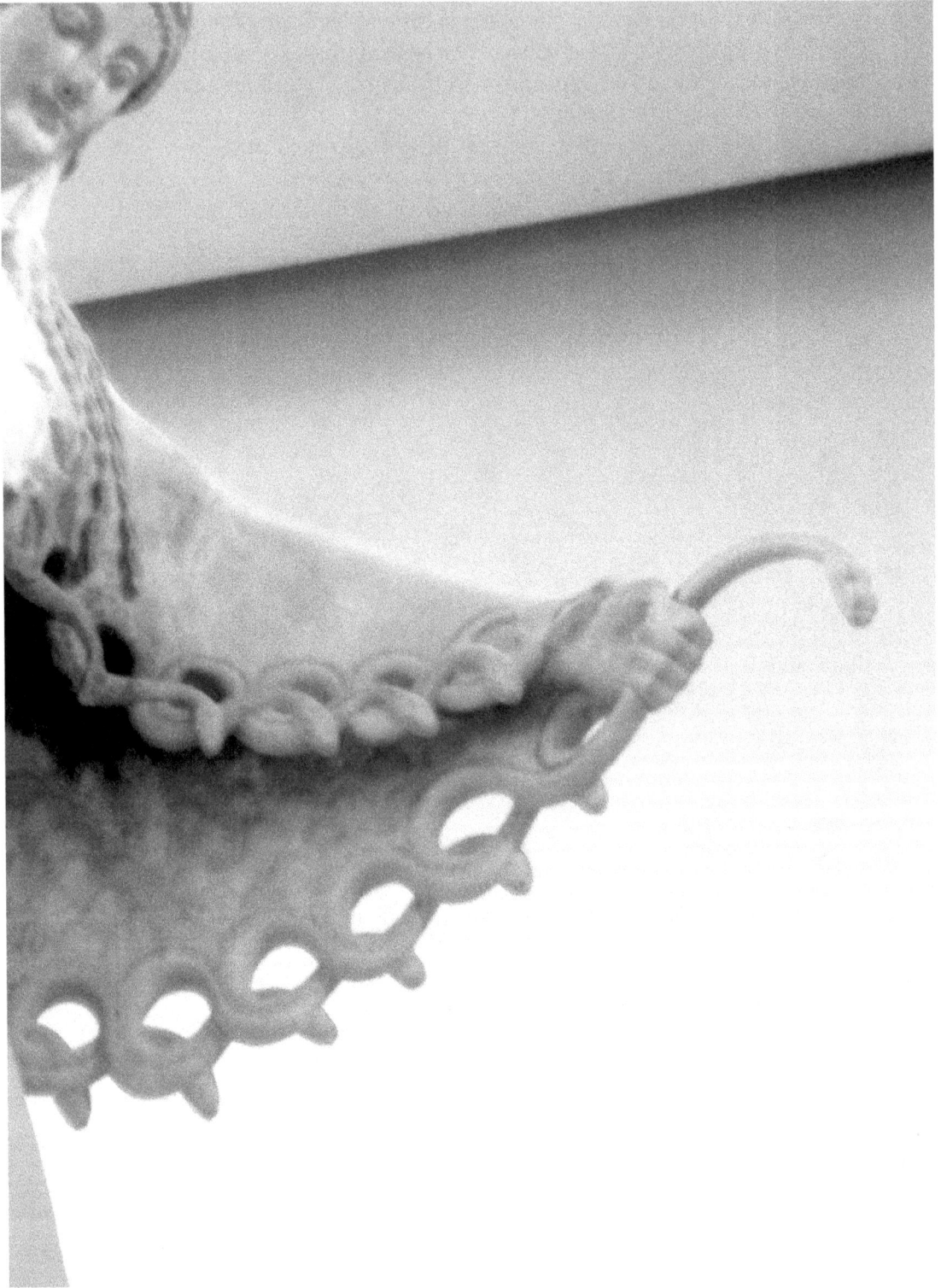

Ritual Stories, Poems, and Dramas

Spring Equinox: Persephone's Garden

By Missy Burchfield

Long ago, in the time when they believed the Earth was flat, in the far reaches of the Greek world, there lived a small and humble farming family. The two girl children, Athanasia and Zenobia knew there was nothing but fields of wheat as far as the eye could see in most every direction-save one. Off to the west grew a stand of trees near a stream, and tucked away in these trees was a very special place, a place the girls called their Secret Garden.

During the hottest days of the year, when all growth ceased and the days were lazy and long, the girls would dream of the seasons when the garden was in bloom. This garden was the very first place where the flowers would return as well as the last from which they would depart every year.

One such day, after months of heavy heat, the girls' mother said to them, "Young ones, your chores are done. Go out now and play. There is naught to do in here but sit around and be food for the bugs. Find yourselves a shady spot and dream of the rains."

Athanasia, the elder of the two at eleven, smiled freely at the suggestion. She beckoned to her sister with a wink, "Come, Zenobia. Let us see if we can find a suitable place to play."

So off the girls went, following a winding path of their own creation to their most Sacred place, Their Secret Garden. Though there had been no flowers for three months now, the girls were careful always to check for weeds and keep everything in order. They took great pride in their work, but they also guarded their secret fiercely. Their Father, though he meant well, could be a little over protective, and the girls were fearful that he would disallow their trips to the Garden if he ever found out.

Because they were so careful with their treasured knowledge, the girls were very surprised not only to find their Garden blooming, but also to see a woman standing among the dripping rose bushes with a bloom in her hand. Frozen in their tracks, they barely flinched when the woman locked eyes with them and smiled warmly.

"Excuse me," Athanasia finally spoke. "We did not mean to disturb you."

"Nonsense," the woman replied. "You must be the ones who have been caring for my garden in my absence."

Zenobia frowned in confusion. "Your Garden?" she asked. "How come I have never seen you here before?"

The woman laughed. "I live very far away, but this is one of my most favorite places in all of Hellenismos."

"Mine, too!" exclaimed Zenobia.

"What are your names, if I may ask?" inquired the lady.

"I'm Zenobia, and I'm five and a half," Zenobia declared. "And that's Athanasia. She's eleven and thinks she's a grown up."

The Lady bowed her head slightly and said, "Pleased to make your acquaintance. My name is Persephone."

Both girls gaped at her in astonishment. They were simple country children, but not completely unawares of the religion of the Great City, infused as it was in everything they did. But the girls knew the story of Persephone and Hades. Persephone was the Dark Queen of the Underworld, not a beautiful woman in a garden.

"Judging by your stunned silence, I would wager you have at least heard my name before?" Persephone asked.

"But, Persephone is a dark and scary lady who spends her time bossing dead people around. She doesn't like flowers!" Zenobia blurted out. Athanasia stayed her sister and waited.

Persephone regarded this for a moment before she answered her. "Child, in your many years here with us, have you not lost one whom you loved?" Persephone asked.

Athanasia answered for them both, for not long ago they lost their grandmother, the dearest in their hearts. "Our Grandmother now resides in your world."

"I see," said Persephone. "And she was good to you, wasn't she?"

"O, yes!" Zenobia smiled at her memory. "She made the best cakes and told us stories. She is the one who told us about you."

"I am glad to hear of it." Persephone replied walking closer to the children. "Little one, do you think your grandmother, who was wise and kind, would be someplace bad and scary for the rest of eternity?"

"Well, I..." For the first time, Zenobia was unsure what to say.

Athanasia waited, regarding the Goddess carefully as she stood before them. She found her unnerving. More than a little too quickly she said, "Please, we meant no harm. Let us be on our way, and we will not bother your garden again."

"Athanasia, the point I am making is this:" Persephone began. "I may be Queen of the Underworld for a portion of the year, but I am still the Maiden of the Spring when the rains come and wake the Earth. My mother, Demeter, cries freely tears of joy each year when I am given to her again. But while I am away, and she is lost in her longing, the world turns dry and hot and no flowers will grow. It is during this time that I am down below, not in a dark and scary place, as you describe it, but in a warm and comfortable place where your grandmother has come to make her eternal home. And, where ever I go, the flowers follow..." Persephone pointed to the path she walked to reach the children's side, and lo, the way was marked with blooms of every color, as the flowers bloomed at her feet.

Amazement covered the girls' faces. Zenobia's mouth gaped in awe, and Athanasia's eyes were wide with wonder. Persephone continued, "This garden is the

140

last place I see before I go to Hades' side, and the first place to which I come when I return. This is why the flowers here are the last as well as the first.

"Now, since you have admitted freely it was you who has been tending my garden, I must give you your due," said Persephone with a wink. "I know a great deal more than you may think about what goes on in my absence.

"I will be going north soon, but there is magic here that you may use to aid your family. Take you these flowers and make wreaths out of them. Then, take them to your Father's shed. Whatever tools you hang them on will be fruitful in their work upon the Earth. Gaia knows they are my flowers and will bless the tools they have touched. Your father's garden will grow and grow, and your faithfulness will be rewarded to your entire village."

Just then, a chariot drawn by two magnificent horses landed from the sky. They paused long enough for Persephone to gracefully climb into the back, and then off they went, up and away, to carry her to her mother's waiting arms.

Several minutes passed before the girls were able to tear their eyes away from the place where the horses had disappeared into the skyline. Finally, Athanasia returned to herself and regarded Zenobia. "Come, little one, and I will show you how to weave a wreath."

Together, the girls made a dozen wreaths, growing more anxious and excited as they worked. On their way home, they decided still to keep the gift from the Goddess to themselves, lest it didn't work, for they did not wish to lose their garden visits for naught.

They continued to tend the garden whenever they could steal away, and over time, they noticed something very peculiar. All of the seeds their father planted had sprung forth, and much sooner than the neighboring fields. As the season waxed, their father's fields continued to be larger and fuller than all those surrounding them. The neighbors were all in awe over his newly found luck in farming.

Once the harvest arrived, the girls decided to tell their father of what they had done. As the girls spoke, a single tear ran down his face. When the girls were done telling their tale, he quietly asked them to take him to their garden. Once there, he fell to his knees and began to thank the Goddess for her kindness. After some time spent in this manner, he walked slowly around the garden and with an eye keener to the keeping of growing things, tended the areas in need of further work.

The next year, and every year after that, the family spent much time caring for the gardens and following Persephone's instructions. And every year the family farm grew larger and larger. Poverty was no longer a familiar word in their neighborhood, and the children grew up healthy and happy.

Persephone was not seen again, but the evidence of her time in the garden was always there for anyone with the eyes to see the path she walked through the plants, for it was always laced with the largest blooms.

Beltaine: The Punishment of Rhiannon

The story of Rhiannon's punishment and Pryderi's return to her is both tragic and redemptive, tugging at the heartstrings and offering the joy of reunion of mother and child. It is also slightly more mature in subject matter than many of our other seasonal stories, but no less appropriate for the high day of Beltaine.

The Punishment of Rhiannon

By Anivair

They say I killed my son. Killed and ate him. What kind of mother could do that?

And yet here I sit, punished, humiliated, mourning. I've told the tale so many times that I no longer know whether or not I'm guilty. I think ... I don't think I did it. I couldn't. But I will tell you the story all the same.

Years ago I was engaged to an angry and wealthy man called Gwawl. But my heart found another called Pwyll. He was handsome of face and noble of heart. I led him on a horse chase, appearing to ride just faster than his knights so he and I could be alone. I let him catch me and we fell immediately in love. But breaking an engagement was no small task. There was a lot of trickery involved and Pwyll almost ruined it for us ... but that's another story.

A year and a day after our first meeting, Pwyll and I were married. Two years passed before the people started to talk about an heir. They wanted Pwyll to take another wife because I hadn't given him one. So I gave them what they asked for. They were so impatient, but we did what they wanted all the same.

And so I gave birth to a son. And he was perfect. He had my skin and his father's eyes and I loved him more than anything. Holding him in my arms was unlike anything I could have imagined. His breathing, his soft skin, all of it made me want to protect him and give him a perfect world.

I'm sure of all of that. And then ... in the night I gave him to my ladies in waiting. They were to take turns tending to him so that I could sleep. And I was grateful but ... then I woke up with the metallic taste of blood in my mouth. My hands and mouth were covered in it and there were bones lying around me. Little tiny bones. I remembered nothing, but the ladies in waiting ... they said that I had killed my son. That I had eaten my own son. And I knew I hadn't...or I thought I knew. Pwyll believed that I was innocent, of course, but no one else did. Pwell wouldn't kill me, but the people demanded recompense. So he sentenced me.

And I sit here by the gate all day every day. And when people come to the court, as you have done, I tell them this story. I tell them what a monster I am and I have begun to believe it myself. Sometimes they strike me. Sometimes they spit on me or worse. And then I offer to carry them to the court on my back. And often they let me. Some take no small satisfaction in treating me like a beast of burden. But I let them. I carried them all the way to Pwyll's castle, where my home used to be.

That was my life, and while it takes a lot to make a goddess question her sanity, I did. I wondered, often, if I had done it. Everyone seemed so sure. And I served that penance for seven long years, a goddess doing work lower than that of a servant.

Until one day. Two men came, one old and one young. And I told them my story. Not as I just told you. By the end of seven years, I had no feeling left in it and I didn't even bother to defend myself. And they nodded and didn't judge me. The old man smiled a bit. And I asked them if they wanted to be carried. They said no, but told me to come with them anyway. And so I did. I was little more than a slave by then.

The man was Teyrnon. When we got to the castle he asked to see Pwyll and he told us both his tale.

He told us that every year a beast had come to his nearby farm to take his newborn foals and that seven years ago he had been ready for the beast. He'd killed it and cut open its belly, and found a baby boy inside. And he had taken the child, and cleaned him, and raised him. He told us that the man beside him was that boy, grown to adulthood in just seven years. He knew that his child was not a mortal then and when he heard my story he knew that the child was my son. I renamed him Pryderi, which means care, in honor of the care Teyrnon had shown him.

There are no words for what I felt on that day. To have my name and my sanity returned to their rightful place was more than I could have hoped for. But to be reunited with my son, the small being I had wept for, mourned and felt such guilt over. I no longer felt like a shadow of myself. The purpose to my suffering was for this moment. I saw life around me for the first time in seven years. Flowers springing forth as they had without my knowing for years, greeting the joyous return of my son. The season's colts ran around us. Life as I had forgotten was suddenly clear again and my family was reunited and restored.

And now, with every year, the plants come forth and begin to grow. The fawns are born and my people begin their labor for the bountiful harvest. This is the time of year when you can look around you and feel life and realize that it has returned to the world. The new life springs up around us while we are not paying attention. It was on a day like this, that my name and my family were restored and all was right with the world.

On this day, when you see the new life around you and you feel the warmth of the season and celebrate it, I would ask that you think of me and remember my story.

Remember that even in the darkest of times, there is hope whether we believe it or not. Take comfort all year in this season, because it will always return to you as my son and my life were returned to me.

Summer Solstice: Taranis and Sulis

Generally, we don't have any issue with invocations getting the "point" across to our attendees, but we're also not out in so public a place where the folk have never heard of us before. So instead of going all "high church" on the folk who might

143

stumble into our ritual that morning (and I do mean "stumble". . . ComFest is known for its beer), I opted to go "children's story time" on them.

The night before the ritual, I sat down with my books and started looking for information about Sulis (the sun) and Taranis (the thunderer). I make no bones about the fact that we don't have a lot of actual *fact* to go on regarding Gaulish divinities, and so I often feel free to borrow liberally from what's available in the IE world. That night, it was A. A. MacDonnell's *Vedic Mythology* that got my attention.

Under Surya's entry, the sun in the Vedas, I found a small note: There is a story about how Indra stole the wheel of the sun's chariot. I took this and began to work forward.

Some aspects of the story are common themes: the cross-dressing (though it's very muted) of the Thunder God; the image of Dawn as a maiden, blushing *just in case* anyone sees her; the world as bounded by waters on all sides; and the creation of a rainbow as a sort of promise are all things you find just about everywhere. I sort of riffed on those themes, not quite sure where the story would go, and found myself writing it mostly without pause from start to finish, not quite knowing how it would end, myself.

As I wrote the story, I found myself writing from deep within my heart. Particularly at the forefront of my mind were some of my own relationships with very strong, beautiful women, and the feeling that sometimes, others forget that there's just so much more to them than a beautiful face.

In the end, the story is one part ancient mythology, one part creativity, and one part mythologizing the women I love so deeply because of their fathomless inner strengths. I would name them now, but I don't particularly want to embarrass them (or leave any of them out!). The central action of Sulis carrying the chariot, and her beauty being in her strength of character and knowledge of what is right, as well as its unexpected but true nature, is the key to this story, in my mind.

The Stolen Wheel

By Rev. Michael J Dangler

It is said that long ago, when even the gods were young, Taranis, the Thunderer, saw Sulis, the Sun, bathing at dawn.

Each morning, Sulis would rise from the cosmic waters at the edge of the world. As she rose from the waters, she would blush deeply, and only a glimpse of her could be seen as she ascended into her chariot. No man was allowed to look upon her, for she was young and beautiful, untouched.

Once she had mounted her chariot, whose wheel is the sun, she would ride all day, the wheel shining brightly as it turned along the path, until she returned once again to her bath in the cosmic waters, the *aquae sulis*.

The god Taranis had heard of her beauty, and though he knew that it was not allowed, he went one morning to see her bathe. Cloaked in his stormclouds to hide his form, he went down to the waters' edge. Taranis was not subtle, however, and Sulis refused to leave the waters.

"Who is there?" she called out.

Thinking quickly, he disguised his voice. "It is I, Epona's handmaiden, come to see your horses."

"But there is nothing wrong with my horses," Sulis responded, puzzled.

"My Lady fears one may be lame. Let me check them while you prepare for your journey."

Sulis agreed, knowing now that it was no man, but a maiden who had come to visit her. As Taranis hid beneath his cloak of clouds, Sulis exited the waters. Instantly, he was struck with lust, and plotted to see more of her.

"How are my horses?" Sulis asked.

"They are fine, my dear," answered Taranis. "Now, be on your way."

And so Taranis watched in awe as she passed by him, wondering how he might see her, so beautiful and naked, again. She mounted the chariot, flicked her reins, and disappeared behind the bright, shining sun wheel.

Taranis knew he must see her again. To do this, he left and flew to the west, intent on stealing the wheel of the sun, for he could not look upon her while the wheel shone so brightly.

He set his ambush far away, placing his clouds in the sky in the west, knowing that she could only travel a fixed path. He waited until the afternoon, and then began to approach the chariot of the sun.

He cast wide his cloak of clouds, racing forth in his own thundering chariot, obscuring the light of Sulis by covering the wheel. He stole the wheel from the axle and hid it deep within the folds of his cloak, laughing peels of thunder at his cleverness.

But Sulis was no weak woman. She was far-seeing and knew things beyond earth, sea and sky. She knew her path, though the cloak of clouds was dark, and she called on the horses to follow it. As the horses pulled, she dismounted the chariot and lifted the axle on her own, carrying it forth, becoming bright herself in the process. Taranis was once again blinded, though this time it was with a beauty born of strength unexpected.

When Taranis saw this, he was in awe—so beautiful a goddess, and yet so strong in her own right. Ashamed, he averted his eyes, admitted the spying, and replaced the wheel. He set Sulis gently on her chariot, and began to ride his away.

As Sulis became once again visible in the daylight sky, and the clouds receded, Taranis offered one final apology: he reflected the inner light of Sulis' beauty, and brought us the rainbow, the most magnificent display of fire in water.

Children of the earth, this is the story of the Wheel of the Sun, how the Thunderer stole it, and the beauty of his apology to an underestimated woman.

Lughnassadh: The Marriage of Lugus and Rosmerta

Written for the Three Cranes Grove, ADF, 2007 Summer Solstice ritual, this poem was written more as the script for a play than anything else. While the poem was recited, actors portrayed the parts of Lugus and Rosmerta (and a few warriors). It was designed mostly to simply tell the story (as best as can be reconstructed). Special thanks are in order to Mary Jones, whose *Celtic Encyclopedia* is ever useful, and to Ariotanos, whose *Outline of Neo-Gaulish Religion and Culture (v. 7)* continues to inform a lot of our ideas about working Gaulish religion.

The Marriage of Lugus and Rosmerta
By Rev. Michael J Dangler

In ancient days when the world was young
the land herself sought out her king.
She called out to the tribes to send
forth all their best and noblest.

In bouts of skill and strength and word
did each compete and each excel,
but in the end one man arose
and stood apart from all the rest.

His eyes shone clear, his shoulders broad,
but gentle was his temperament.
Of kingly bearing he was made;
there was no question here of that.

His name was Lugus, Giant's Bane,
his strength and honor unsurpassed;
he knew the many arts of man
and worked them all with skillful hand.

The land, Rosmerta, called him near
and held aloft a cup of mead.
"This cup," she said, "is all my love,
and in it find your sovereignty."

His hands reached forth and grasped the cup;
Rosmerta, though, did not let go
and held the cup firm in her hands:
"There is one thing before you drink."

"The people first approve their king,
by their consent his rule is whole,
for he serves them for all his days,
and should he fail, they'll have his head."

And to the people she called out,
"The land rejects an unjust king:
Will you hold to this mighty oath?"
And how do th'folk respond to her?
(the folk: "We do!")

And to the people she called out,
"And if your king should be unjust,
then do you swear to throw him out?"
And how do th'folk respond to her?
(the folk: "We do!")

And to the people she called out,
"Do you, dear people, love the land,
and do you hold my honor bright?"
And how do th'folk respond to her?
(the folk: "We do!")

Rosmerta now released the cup
and Lugus drank the mead so sweet.
The Land had found her champion,
and the people had found a king.

Hail to Lugus, the rightful king!
Hail to Rosmerta who chose him!
Hail to the folk who give him leave,
and ever have power o're him!

Autumnal Equinox: *Clutiā Trion Garanonon*

"The Fame of Three Cranes"

It is a long-standing Three Cranes tradition to add a stanza to our Grove poem each year for our Autumnal Equinox anniversary rite. That stanza is added as the second-to-last stanza. This tradition was started by Rev. Jenni Hunt, our Grove's first ranked bard, and it charts our history beautifully. We hope to continue this tradition for many, many years, and we hope that the bards of Three Cranes, as well as the bards of ADF, will keep this poem in their memories and will tell it to others.

This poem is both praise and prayer for our Grove, calling out to the "gardener" of our folk, here named "Teutates" – a name that simply means "god of our tribe." To us, Teutates is truly the god of our folk, as we have always encouraged our members to understand him (or her) in the way they see fit.

This is the version given at the Three Cranes Grove, ADF, Autumnal Equinox ritual, in 2009, and the poem is kept up-to-date on our website. Special thanks to Deiniol Jones for his help with the title translation.

"Clutiā Trion Garanonon"
The Fame of Three Cranes
by the Members of Three Cranes Grove, ADF

Once scattered kernels, random strewn,
Unfertilized, asleep, unkissed,
Lethargic, lurking, latent bloom
Columbus craved a catalyst.

New generation, gumption aimed
Its fertile minds and thirsting souls
Have rooted grove, Three Cranes benamed.
Its spate of growth this Bard extols.

By Kindred sown, a seedling stand
The budding beauty sprouted, surged.
Assisted by the gardener's hand,
Its roots grew deep, its branches merged.

New fruit of labors just begun
With common vision splices hearts;
Enlightened minds may meld as one—
The whole is greater than its parts.

With blood and sweat Cranes served with mirth;
We honored Buffett, Saturn, Soul,
Toys, canned goods, banners, growth in girth
The Gods screamed, "Grow into your role!"

Three years' new rings; we're in a groove—
A teenage tree with growing pains,
Its awkwardness we need improve
And root into pristine terrains.

Through angry waters and winds of change
As one we light communion flames
Our course is chartered; our branches reach
Our bards and brewers are awarded fame

Our leaves stretch forth to shelter friends,
Blessings abound: the omens good.
One Priest called forth, one Priest called home,
Strengthening Ghosti, as we should.

Each moon we meet 'neath robur's crown,
And celebrate what members bring.
Through work and deed our voices sound:
We stand as one, our gardens sing

Our trunk grows strong, our numbers soared:
Through fifty rites we've served our folk!
Transforming ways we're moving toward,
Wrapped tightly in Crane-feathered cloak.

Teutates, consecrate Three Cranes,
Electrify us to the core
With fire inspire; with nurturing rains
Suffuse us, drench us one year more!

Additional Modules

Seamus' version of the Waters of Life

Seamus wrote this after Rev. Michael J Dangler gave an overview of his reasoning on the Waters of Life at a Liturgy Meeting. Mike has a very clear 9-step litany for the Waters of Life. Seamus used his rough outline and many of his words because they are familiar to our Grove. He also added his own spin on things that he had either read from Ian and Skip or seen in rituals.

Waters of Life

We have shared praises and given scarifies; we have enjoyed fellowship and built community. Our voices have resounded in the well, echoed in the trees, and have been carried on the flames. We have honored the Ancient and Mighty Ones and they have honored us with the omens in return.

These omens are powerful ones. I ask that we take a minute to relax and take a deep breath and reflect on these omens. Think about these blessings and how they affect you.

Also think about how they affect this Grove of people and the greater community…do not allow these omens to be wasted, blown away on the wind, take them into your heart, record them there and reflect on them daily, allow them to resound in your daily life.

Once again I ask that you take a deep breath, and in your mind's eye see the blessings take form and manifest. A mist surrounds us and there is one single ray of light shining down from the heavens or a deep welling from the bosom of the earth…see the blessings in your own way, and know that the kindred pour out for you.

By its very nature water is sacred, it is our life's blood, it is what sustains us and all of the Mother's creatures. It flows through our veins like the rivers of our Mother…

It is the prayer for and prayer against, whether it is the dry parched days of drought or the unending rain that causes the swelling of the floods, there is no denying the power of water. Welling up or falling from the sky…

Today we separate these waters and consecrate them, asking that they be infused with the blessings of the Kindreds. (Pour water and place between candles)

Ancient and Mighty Ones, we have honored you and you have offered us blessings in return. *Shining Ones give us the waters*. (Light 1st candle)

Noble ones, your blessings mingle with the water before us infusing them, becoming one with them. *Shining Ones give us the waters*. (Light 2nd candle)

Shining Ones, may your blessings come in all ways, in all forms, mixing first with these Waters and then in our lives. Shining bright with your love for us: *Shining Ones give us the waters*. (Light 3rd candle)

(Take a minute to direct the blessings into the water then hold waters above head)

Behold the Waters of Life!

Children of the Earth, in this time of magic, you are offered these blessings. Before you is the holy cup, do you wish to share in these blessings?

Do you come in honor of the old ways?

Do you desire that each and all of us be blessed?

Then drink deep in wisdom, strength and blessings!

(Waters are passed out)

We have shared in the Waters, the outpourings of the blessings from the Kindreds. Feel those Waters within you. Feel the blessings start to shine and manifest. We have been blessed. Let us now turn to our workings. . .

Waters Module

By Rev. Michael J Dangler

Endless are the Waters
  Joyfully flowing
  Thoroughly cleansing
  Never sleeping
Endlessly flowing in channels
  Furrowed by Taranis
  The Great Bull
  The Thunderer
Shining Ones, give us the Waters!

These are the Waters from the Heavens
  Waters from the Earth
  Waters gushing free.
Alone, Shining Waters
  Roaring in blessings
  Beautifully flowing to the ocean
Shining Ones, give us the Waters!

Presiding over the flowing Waters
  Are the Shining Ones
  Who know truth from falsehood.
Shining Ones, givers of Blessing
  Knowers of cosmic order
  Ceaselessly purifying
Shining Ones, give us the Waters!

Opening the Gates – Nine Worlds

By Anna Gail

Gatekeepers:

Mighty Norns, Urd Verdandi, Skud
Thurs maidens of what was, what is and what may be
You are the weavers of Wyrd
You are the carvers of Örlög
You are the deliverers of destiny to god and man alike.
You are the Jotun maids that the gods seek council from
You are the guardians of the well of Urd
You are the nourishers of Yggdrasil, the world tree.
You who touch all 9 realms
Wise ones, we honor you and ask you to stand as guardians of the gates.
Blend your magic with ours that none may cause harm to those gathered here
Help us as we open the gates and tred the ancient paths
Ladies of the Ash, accept our offering with hail and welcome!

Opening the Gates:

To the realm of Asgard - land of the Aesir and the Asyniur
Hear our call while this flame burns bright (light candle)
Open wide your gates and join the children of the old ways.

To the realm of Vanaheim - land of the Vanir
Hear our call while this flame burns bright (light candle)
Open wide your gates and join the children of the old ways.

To the realm of Alfheim - land of the Alvs and the Alfar
Hear our call while this flame burns bright (light candle)
Open wide your gates and join the children of the old ways.

To the realm of Midgard - land of man and landvettir
Hear our call while this flame burns bright (light candle)
Open wide your gates and welcome those of the old ways

To the realm of Muspelheim - land of fire and one force of creation
Hear our call while this flame burns bright (light candle)
Open wide your gates and join the children of the old ways.

To the realm of Jotunheim - land of the Jotunar
Hear our call while this flame burns bright (light candle)
Open wide your gates and join the children of the old ways.

To the realm of Helheim - land of the dead and our Disir
Hear our call while this flame burns bright (light candle)
Open wide your gates and join the children of the old ways.

To the realm of Niflheim - land of ice and the second force of creation
Hear our call while this flame burns bright (light candle)
Open wide your gates and join the children of the old ways.

To the realm of Svartalfheim - land of dark elves and forgers of treasure
Hear our call while this flame burns bright (light candle)
Open wide your gates and join the children of the old ways.

9 realms we have called
9 doors we knocked upon
9 flames we burn
Let the gates be open!

Closing the Gates:

To the realm of Svartalfheim
You joined our rite while this flame burned (douse flame)
Close now your gates with thanks from the children of the old ways

To the realm of Niflheim
You joined our rite while this flame burned (douse flame)
Close now your gates with thanks from the children of the old ways

To the realm of Helheim
You joined our rite while this flame burned (douse flame)
Close now your gates with thanks from the children of the old ways

The realm of Jotunheim
You joined our rite while this flame burned (douse flame)
Close now your gates with thanks from the children of the old ways

To the realm of Muspelheim
You joined our rite while this flame burned (douse flame)
Close now your gates with thanks from the children of the old ways

To the realm of Alfheim
You joined our rite while this flame burned (douse flame)
Close now your gates with thanks from the children of the old ways

To the realm of Vanaheim
You joined our rite while this flame burned (douse flame)
Close now your gates with thanks from the children of the old ways

To the realm of Asgard
You joined our rite while this flame burned (douse flame)
Close now your gates with thanks from the children of the old ways

To the realm of Midgard
As we dwell within your borders we do not close this gate.
Instead we put out this flame with hail and thanks to those of the old ways. (douse flame)

9 realms we honored
9 doors we shut
9 flames burned out
Let the gates be closed!

Gatekeepers:

Urd, Verdandi, Skud
Norns of Yggdrasil
Our gatekeepers and guarders of fate
The children of the old ways honor you for your work done here.
Go now in peace with our hail and thanks.

Two Powers – Convection

By Anne Delekta

This version of the two powers meditation/attunement uses the power of convection, with cold energy coming from the sky and hot energy from the earth. It was originally used in the Grove's Imbolc liturgy in 2007.

Plant your feet firmly, and draw your spine up straight. Inhale deeply and fully, feeling your belly expand. Pause briefly, feeling the fullness of your lungs. Now exhale completely, tightening your belly as you expel the air from your lungs. Pause here, at the bottom of the breath, experiencing the emptiness of your lungs. Again, let us inhale deeply, pause briefly, then exhale fully, and pause. And a third time, let us inhale, pause, exhale, pause.

Now allow your breath to settle into its normal pattern, breathing in and out through your nose if you are able.

We stand together, in this place, on this earth, where we have come to worship the gods. Our breaths mingle in the air around us, and our feet share the earth.

Extend your awareness down into the earth, through the cold soil and rock and bedrock, down until you reach the molten outer core of the earth. Here is the fire at the belly of our planet, and here is the molten heat of Brigando's forge. Pull the liquid heat of the forge up from the depths, draw it up through your legs, and feel the molten energy pool in the cauldron of your pelvis. Feel the energy swirl through you, and pull it higher into your body, swirling through your belly, and higher, until it pools in the vessel of your heart. Feel it pulse and swirl, always moving, and feel it extend out through your arms and up through your throat, into your head, where it swirls and flows, rises and descends, and sinuously glides within us. Now raise your hands and place them on the crown of your head, feeling the complete circuit of hot earth energy moving within you, coming up from the earth, and flowing back into the earth, yet constantly filling you.

Now raise your hands to the sky, and feel the vastness of the heavens above us. Push your awareness up, up, and up beyond the air, beyond the clouds, and into the coldness and darkness of space. Plunge your hands into the depths of the universe, and pull the cold, dark energy of space down from above, down through the sky, down to meet the hot fluid energy of earth. Feel the cold energy of space flow down through your hands, through the crown of your head, feel it flow through and around the molten energy of earth. Both energies move and flow and pulse; the hot energy coming up from the earth seeks to rise, while the cold energy from space seeks to descend. The energies move together, pulsing, flowing, creating currents and eddies within ourselves. Move your body gently side to side, feeling the pulse of energies in that physical movement. Gradually still the movements, but feel the energy as it continues to flow and move within you. Extend your hands to grasp those beside you. Where cold and heat meet, the two merge into flexible strength. We are strong with the powers of earth and sky, of hot forge and quenching cold; we stand together and strong, united by the universal energies that fill us.

Now let us open our eyes, and prepare to worship the gods.

Two Powers – Crocus Meditation

By Rev. Jenni Hunt

This Two Powers meditation was done at our first Imbolc ritual, and is affectionately referred to as "the crocus meditation" within the Grove.

Imbolc Two Powers Meditation

Close your eyes and stand firmly rooted to the Earth. Take a deep breath and feel the cold. Exhale a small cloud of frozen breath. Take a few moments to focus on the bitter cold. When you inhale, the icy chill fills your lungs, making you shiver and your teeth chatter.

You may have felt at times during the past week that you'd never been so cold, that you may never be warm again. You've noticed the days getting longer, but it still just keeps getting colder and colder.

See yourself as a bare, shivering tree on the top of windswept, craggy hill. The wind whistles through your bare branches, bending you back with its bitter, chill gusts until you think you will crack and be swept away.

But your strong roots firmly grasp the rocks and frozen ground. You are firmly embedded and will not be swept away. Feel those roots stretch down past the rock, down past the frosty soil and down into the warm, life-giving bosom of the Earth. Draw that warmth and life up through your roots, up through the frozen ground and rocks, up into your feet and legs, warming you and giving you energy, up through your groin and belly, warming your chest, flowing and warming your shoulders, arms and hands. Roll your neck and shoulders as the warm Earth waters flow up through your neck and head.

You notice now that the sun has come out from behind the clouds, and you squint as its bright, distant heat warms your crown and mixes with the moist warmth from below. The sun grows stronger, and you feel its warmth on your face, warming your shoulders and arms, spreading down your back and filling your breast, swirling with the warm waters from below into your groin, down through your legs and into your feet.

Chill though the wind may be, you draw warmth, light and life from below and above.

With your mind's eye, look around you on this cold, craggy hilltop. Steam rises up from the frozen ground at your feet, as the snow is melted from below and above. As you feel yourself thawing from the warmth that emanates from above and below, the warm vapor begins to dissipate from the air, the snow at your feet melts away and sinks down into the Earth, carrying with it the warm energy from the Sun, and the Earth pushes up from below a single, perfect crocus, living proof of the return of warmth from both below and above.

You realize now that you are not alone on this hilltop, with nothing at all to break the bitter wind. There are others just like you all around, bare-branched and frozen nearly to the marrow. Without this grove of trees, you would indeed have been naked to the elements. Without those surrounding you, there would have been no windbreak to protect you, alone, at the mercy of the cold.

We stand, as a grove, greater than the sum of our parts.

Book Attunement

By Seamus

Take a moment, relax…find your center….shake off the worries of the day. Breath deep. Exhale fully…pushing out all the cares, worries and distractions of the day.

Breathe deep a second time, breath in the air of our sacred grove, charged with the energy of anticipation and potential.

Stand firm and feel the pulse of our Mother Earth surge up through the soles of your feet.

Stand rooted now…

In your mind's eye see yourself moving through time and space, with the energies of potential swirling around you. Until suddenly you stop and find yourself in a sacred grove of trees.

In the middle of the grove stands an old stone altar, sitting on the altar is a huge leather bound book. The book is well worn and on the cover you see stamped or carved into the leather the symbol of the world tree.

Reach out now and open the book. The first page is filled with a picture. Not just an ordinary picture, not stagnate and frozen in time, but a moving picture.

The scene depicts a time long, long ago. The beginnings of our mother earth. You see a dry barren land, devoid of life. You see in the distance the molten rivers of lava as it rolls and bubbles forward. All around you see and feel the energy of potential. You scan the horizon and in the distant blood red sky you see black rolling thunderheads stumbling across the day. You see lightning flash and then you see the first rain. The original waters of life. The rain comes, pounding the ground, cooling the lava. Steam raises, mist rolls out and as you continue to gaze into the picture the wind catches the pages of the book flipping them forward. Several pages ahead it flips until the wind dies and the pages stop.

Again you see the same basic picture, but now the skies are blue, and the barren land has been replaced with the rolling green meadows and deep blue water. And there in the center of the frame stands a tree. The sacred oak. Standing young, tall and proud. The bilé…As you look closer you see two acorns. One for Dagda and the second for Brigit…and in these acorns we again see the seeds of potential. Once again the wind catches the pages of the book. And as the pages flip by and began to settle, you see the faces of those around you and then the pages settle on a picture of…..you.

And it dawns on you that as in the beginning, as in those long ago seeds of potential, that same DNA is in you. That same potential swirls in you. Tap into that energy now, allow yourself to become the sacred oak. Allow the waters of life that we share today to nourish that potential. And give you direction. Reach out once more in your mind's eye and turn the page in the book. To the last page…and there on the final page you see the picture of us here today. All of us standing united. Here we stand as a sacred grove. Teeming with potential. Multiplying the potential of each of us. Becoming greater than the sum of our parts.

May the waters support and surround us, may the land extend about us, may the sky stretch out above us at the center lives a burning flame. May the Kindreds bless us, may our worship be true, may our actions be just, and may our love be pure. Blessings, honor and worship to the holy ones.

Dancing the Maypole

Beltaine 2009

Full Rituals

House Blessing: Anagantios Rite

By Rev. Michael J Dangler

In February, when the weather is blustery and cold, the Grove follows the old Coligny Calendar. There, the festival of Anagantios is listed for the sixth night of the new moon. *Anagantios* translates as "stay-at-home-month," and that's the best thing to do at this time of year.

At our first Druid Moon Rite in February, our Grove Priest, Rev. Dangler, visited seven Grove Members' houses and carried the flame of Brigando from our Imbolc rite through the houses. The flame we use came from Kildare, Brigid's eternal flame. We started using this flame in our Imbolc rites (which are to Brigando), on the general theory that this flame is about the closest we can get to Brigando's own eternal flame (if she ever had one), and Brigid is the patron of enough of our members that it holds some real meaning for our members. This is the ritual we used.

Lighting the Flame

By Rev. Michael J Dangler

This flame was kindled in Kildare,
brought across the Ninth Wave,
and kept here in Columbus by a member of our Grove.
It is the fire of our Imbolc ritual,
the flame of our devotion,
and the Grove's own fire.

Transferring the Flame

By Rev. Michael J Dangler
(heavily influenced by Ceisiwr Serith)

The Fire from the waters is here.
The Fire from the land is here.
The Fire from the heavens is here.
Born in the Waters, Kindled on the Earth,
and with a pillar of smoke that supports the Heavens,
this light is the Grove's own Fire of Sacrifice.

Blessing the House

By Rev. Michael J Dangler
(with heavy input from 3CG members:
Anna Gail, Shawneen, Seamus, and Lees)

From floor to ceiling,
from wall to wall,
from [feature] to [feature];[7]
in all the cracks and crevices and corners,
this light warms and illuminates all.
Let this light warm and illuminate
all who live here or visit here.[8]

Final Blessing

By Rev. Michael J Dangler

[place the candle on the hearth/stove]
From hearth to heart,
from heart to hearth:
here we light a candle from this blessed fire
and give it to those who dwell here.
This flame is the Grove's flame,
kindled at Kildare,
brought across the Ninth Wave,
and kept by a Grove member here in Columbus.
It is the Fire we share,
and the Fire that has now blessed our homes.

[Grove member is given a candle kindled from the flame]

Grove members are also given the instruction to not blow out the candle, but only to snuff it out physically, as these are the instructions we received from Shawneen, who brought the flame to us from across the ocean. This rite could be done without this flame, too, but it would need some additional work to re-work some of the imagery (the "kindled at Kildare, brought across the Ninth Wave" imagery is really cool).

---

[7] "[feature] to [feature]": The "[feature]" should be replaced with something in the room, such as "from bed to dresser" in the bedroom, or "hook to hanger" in a closet, or "stove to sink to cupboard space" in the kitchen. Use the opportunity to mention things in the room that might need a blessing. They don't all have to be serious, either: "from toilet to catbox" was common in bathrooms, because those are things no one wants fouled.

[8] In the kitchen, which is where this rite ended in all cases (well, where there was a kitchen), the last line would change to "all who live or visit or receive hospitality from this place."

The Outdwellers Rite

By Nicholas Egelhoff

In every ADF ritual we honor the Three Kindreds (the Ancestors, the Spirits of the Land, and the Deities), while asking those beings that we call "Outdwellers," who we feel to be at odds and cross-purposes to us and to the Kindreds, to stay out of our ritual, usually by placating them to a degree with some small offering. But just because these Outdwellers may not harmonize with us or the Kindreds very well or that easily, does not mean that they should not receive some respect.

In much of Indo-European myth, especially Old Norse, the generation of deities prior to those that are worshipped commonly by the folk are usually held to be giants and monsters who had to be brought down by the gods of humanity in order for the world and life as we know it to grow and prosper. But in many of the stories, these beings are not seen as intrinsically evil in any common Western/Judeo-Christian sense of morality, in most respects they are seen as too vast, too wild for them to be able rulers over the world of human beings—in many cases they are seen embodied in the mountains, the hurricane, the tornado, the raging wildfire. None of which are evil *per se*, but are still harmful to and uncontrollable by human beings. In this way these primordial deities are seen as the enemies of the gods, who protect and foster humanity, not because they are innately immoral in any way in comparison to the gods or humanity.

And so, as in many tribal cultures, we can find a way to extend a certain level of respect to these beings, if only in the capacity of the "honored enemy." But they also deserve a level of respect beyond just that; we should remember that in many cases, these beings brought forth the manifest universe from the roiling chaos of infinite potential that existed prior to it (even if in many stories the gods remake the universe after they bring down their forebears, these elder deities still gave the universe its early form, which is no small feat). That in and of itself deserves accolades.

That is why I developed the Outdwellers Rite: so that we will not forget those who took the first, monumental steps in shaping the world as we know it and giving us even the scantest chance of existing; so that we will, at the very least, give due honor to our "enemies" and not forget that without them to mirror us, darkly, we would lose a piece of our collective identity.

Materials Recommended: (feel free to adapt as necessary/desired)
- Beer
- Grain
- Eggnog
- Golden Apple with *Καλλιστι* carved into it
- Wine

- A shot of Jack Daniels

Initiating the Rite:
- Musical signal (bells, clapping, etc.).

Purification:
- Cense and/or asperse using sage and/or water.
- Give beer to the Kindreds, asking that they watch over the rite, but do not interfere unless it is absolutely necessary.

Honoring the Earth Mother:
- Offer a prayer to Gaea and give the grain to her.

Statement of Purpose:
- "I am here to honor the Eldest of the Eldest, those who first came forth from the chaos of the beginning and wrenched forth the form of the worlds. Though many be the enemies of the gods, many have joined them in friendship and many have offered up their knowledge and wisdom when it was needed. May respect always be given to those who oppose us, for we will always need them to challenge us and help to define who we are as a people."

(Re)Creating the Cosmos:
- I find it appropriate to read a bit of creation myth that focuses on the *jotuns*, *titans*, etc., explaining their efforts at first shaping the cosmos. I have used parts of Hesiod's *Theogony* (see below), but this is up to the discretion of those performing the ritual.
- "Verily at the first Chaos came to be, but next wide-bosomed Earth, the ever-sure foundations of all the deathless ones who hold the peaks of snowy Olympus, and dim Tartarus in the depth of the wide-pathed Earth, and Eros, fairest among the deathless gods, who unnerves the limbs and overcomes the mind and wise counsels of all gods and all men within them. From Chaos came forth Erebus and black Night; but of Night were born Aether and Day, whom she conceived and bore from union in love with Erebus. And Earth first bore starry Heaven, equal to herself, to cover her on every side, and to be an ever-sure abiding-place for the blessed gods. And she brought forth long Hills, graceful haunts of the goddess-Nymphs who dwell amongst the glens of the hills. She bore also the fruitless deep with his raging swell, Pontus, without sweet union of love. But afterwards she lay with Heaven and bore deep-swirling Oceanus, Coeus and Crius and Hyperion and Iapetus, Theia and Rhea, Themis and Mnemosyne and gold-crowned Phoebe and lovely Tethys. After them was born Cronos the wily, youngest and most terrible of her children, and he hated his lusty sire.

"And again, she bore the Cyclopes, overbearing in spirit, Brontes, and Steropes and stubborn-hearted Arges, who gave Zeus the thunder and made the thunderbolt: in all else they were like the gods, but one eye only was set in the midst of their fore-heads. And they were surnamed Cyclopes because one orbed eye was set in their foreheads. Strength and might and craft were in their works.

"And again, three other sons were born of Earth and Heaven, great and doughty beyond telling, Cottus and Briareos and Gyes, presumptuous children. From their shoulders sprang an hundred arms, not to be approached, and each had fifty heads upon his shoulders on their strong limbs, and irresistible was the stubborn strength that was in their great forms. For of all the children that were born of Earth and Heaven, these were the most terrible, and they were hated by their own father from the first.

"And he used to hide them all away in a secret place of Earth so soon as each was born, and would not suffer them to come up into the light: and Heaven rejoiced in his evil doing. But vast Earth groaned within, being straitened, and she made the element of grey flint and shaped a great sickle, and told her plan to her dear sons. And she spoke, cheering them, while she was vexed in her dear heart:

"'My children, gotten of a sinful father, if you will obey me, we should punish the vile outrage of your father; for he first thought of doing shameful things.'

"So she said; but fear seized them all, and none of them uttered a word. But great Cronos the wily took courage and answered his dear mother:

"'Mother, I will undertake to do this deed, for I reverence not our father of evil name, for he first thought of doing shameful things.'

"So he said: and vast Earth rejoiced greatly in spirit, and set and hid him in an ambush, and put in his hands a jagged sickle, and revealed to him the whole plot.

"And Heaven came, bringing on night and longing for love, and he lay about Earth spreading himself full upon her.

"Then the son from his ambush stretched forth his left hand and in his right took the great long sickle with jagged teeth, and swiftly lopped off his own father's members and cast them away to fall behind him. And not vainly did they fall from his hand; for all the bloody drops that gushed forth Earth received, and as the seasons moved round she bore the strong Erinyes and the great Giants with gleaming armour, holding long spears in their hands and the Nymphs whom they call Meliae all over the boundless earth. And so soon as he had cut off the members with flint and cast them from the land into the surging sea, they were swept away over the main a long time: and a white foam spread around them from the immortal flesh, and in it there grew a maiden. First she drew near holy Cythera, and from there, afterwards, she came to sea-girt Cyprus, and came forth an awful and lovely goddess, and grass grew up about her beneath her shapely feet. Her gods and men call Aphrodite, and the foam-born goddess and rich-crowned Cytherea, because she grew amid the foam, and Cytherea because she reached Cythera, and Cyprogenes because she was born in billowy Cyprus, and Philommedes because sprang from the members. And with her went Eros, and comely Desire followed her at her birth at the first and as she went into the assembly of the gods. This honor she has from the beginning, and this is the portion allotted to her amongst men and undying gods, -- the whisperings of maidens and smiles and deceits with sweet delight and love and graciousness.

"But these sons whom be begot himself great Heaven used to call Titans in reproach, for he said that they strained and did presumptuously a fearful deed, and that vengeance for it would come afterwards.

"And Night bore hateful Doom and black Fate and Death, and she bore Sleep and the tribe of Dreams. And again the goddess murky Night, though she lay with none, bore Blame and painful Woe, and the Hesperides who guard the rich, golden apples and the trees bearing fruit beyond glorious Ocean. Also she bore the Destinies and ruthless avenging Fates, Clotho and Lachesis and Atropos, who give men at their birth both evil and good to have, and they pursue the transgressions of men and of gods: and these goddesses never cease from their dread anger until they punish the sinner with a sore penalty. Also deadly Night bore Nemesis (Indignation) to afflict mortal men, and after her, Deceit and Friendship and hateful Age and hard-hearted Strife.

"But abhorred Strife bore painful Toil and Forgetfulness and Famine and tearful Sorrows, Fightings also, Battles, Murders, Manslaughters, Quarrels, Lying Words, Disputes, Lawlessness and Ruin, all of one nature, and Oath who most troubles men upon earth when anyone wilfully swears a false oath."

Opening the Gates:

- Call upon Ymir as the Gatekeeper, as his body was used to form the *Miðgarð* in Norse myth, he probably has the closest connections to a Gatekeeper among the older generation of deities. If those performing the ritual have a better one in mind, feel free to substitute.
- Offer eggnog (symbolic of the sugary milk of *Auðhumla*) as gift to Ymir.

Inviting the Outdwellers:

- Since the division of Outdwellers isn't as clearly established as it is among the Kindreds, I have divided them in accordance to the region of the worlds they inhabit; change as necessary or desired. For each division, I usually offer a bottle of beer.
- Underworld: Centimani, Cyclopes, *Moðguð*, Hel
- Middle-World: Trolls, Fomorians, Jotnar
- Upper-World: Titans (Prometheus, Epimetheus, etc.), Loki

Key Offerings:

- I have traditionally made Eris the matron of my Outdwellers Rite, but this can be changed as necessary/desired. If one wishes to honor her, the golden apple mentioned above is generally a good offering.
- I have honored Loki as the patron of the rite at least once, using a shot of Jack Daniels Whiskey as an offering (as adapted from the suggestion in *Our Troth, Volume 1*, p. 212).
- For the primordial deities in general, I offer a full bottle of wine.

Prayer of Sacrifice:

- "Mighty Outdwellers, Eldest of the Eldest, and Primordial Deities, accept these offerings!"

Omen:

- I generally use runes. Change as necessary/desired.

(Non-)Calling for Blessing:

- "Mighty and Terrible Ones, I do not ask for a gift in return. You have already given us the gift of a shaped and ordered universe, which you wrought out of the primordial Chaos. We are ever thankful."

Thanking the Outdwellers
Closing the Gates
Thanking the Earth Mother
Closing the Rite

An ADF Oath Rite

By Anna Gail

An Oath Rite is something that you should do as you feel compelled to. It is not to be taken lightly, but only if you are truly compelled to walk the walk. Making an oath is serious business. I chose to do this particular Rite because I felt at this point in my path it was the right course of action, and having completed the work necessary for my Dedicant Path with ADF, it was the last thing I needed to do before submitting everything. I had begun my Paganism journey with totally different deities several years ago. That happens: you can honor more than one, thus polytheism. You do not have to dedicate yourself to a particular deity; rather, you can also dedicate yourself to a particular path. Either way an Oath is important, to yourself, to the cosmos, or to a deity if you incorporate one. It can bring you closer to your path and your gods if you let it.

I.   **Process** ~ Singing "*Come We Now as a People*"

II.   **Outdwellers** ~ an offering to Eris

III.   **Honoring the Earth Mother** ~ Nerthus ~ Singing "*Earth Mother, Blossom Lifter*"

IV.   **Inspiration** ~ Bragi [by Paul Maurice]

> *Bragi, Odinson,*
> *Best of the wordsmiths*
> *And first of the skalds.*
> *You with the tongue of gold*
> *Whose words are like the finest mead,*
> *We ask you best of bards*
> *To bless us and make our words mix well.*
> *Bragi, let your inspiration flow!*

V.   **Honoring the Kindreds**
   a. Ancestors
   b. Landvettir
   c. Aesir & Vanir

VI.   **Gatekeeper** ~ Norns

VII.   **Opening the Gates** ~ 9 realms
   a. Asgard, Vanaheim, Alfheim
   b. Midgard, Jotunheim, Muspelheim
   c. Helheim, Niflheim, Svartalfheim

VIII.   **Honoring Freyja**

IX.   **Oath of dedication**

I enter this sacred space, this meeting place of the nine realms to stand before the Kindreds and my grove mates in honor of the old ways. I, (name inserted here), pledge to honor the gods with my whole heart. To bring offerings in honor of all the kindred, to seek out their blessings. I come to the gates to make an oath of dedication, to follow in the ways of old.

I bring these offerings to Freyja. Vanadis, Goddess of love and war, You who get first pick of the dead, You Mighty Valkyrie, Oh queen of magic hear me and bear witness to this oath. As others before me have done, I come to walk the pagan path, the path of my ancestors. Freyja, Kindreds, let every holy power hear me and may you look with favor upon me as I make my oath.

Hail the Old Ways. Hail the Ancestors, Hail the Landvettir, Hail the Shining Ones.

X.   **Offerings** are made to the three Kindreds to witness the oath

XI.   **The Omen**
   a. One rune is drawn for the Ancestors and given to one seer.

b. One rune is drawn for the Landvettir and given to another seer.

c. One rune is drawn for the Shining Ones and given to a final seer.

d. They interpret and tell me the message

XII. **Waters of Life**

a. Sing "*I drink of the waters of life*" in rounds while the mead is blessed

b. The participants continue the rounds until the horn is filled then end the song with one last round all of us together.

c. "Behold the waters of life"

d. The oath-taker walks up to each person, and asks the following four questions before they drink:

    i. Do you bear witness to my oath?

    ii. Do you agree to hold me to my oath?

    iii. Do you accept the blessings offered by the Kindreds?

    iv. Do you agree to share in these blessings?

e. The horn is then passed to the next person who asks the one making the oath the following before passing the horn on:

    i. Do you agree to stand true to your oath?

f. The next person asks the following before passing it on:

    i. Do you accept the blessings offered by the Kindreds?

g. The last person asks the oath-taker the following

    i. Do you agree to share in these blessings?

h. All three ladies hold the horn out to me to accept and drink from.

i. The rest of the mead is offered to Freyja.

XIII. **Ending of ritual**

a. Thank Freyja

b. Close the gates (in reverse order by person who opened)

c. Thank the gatekeeper

d. Thank the Kindred in reverse order by person who welcomed

e. Thank Bragi for warding our words

f. Thank the Earth Mother and dismiss all participants

"This rite is ended."

The Katrina Rite

By Rev. Jenni Hunt

    After the devastation of Hurricane Katrina in 2005, ADF set up a fund called "ADF Cares" to help raise money for disaster relief and recovery. An important part of ADF's response to the Hurricane was our spiritual response, epitomized by what we now call "The Katrina Rite." Rev. Jenni Hunt wrote this ritual and invited the Grove to come out to perform it with her.

The rite was performed in Goodale Park in Columbus, and in several other places where ADF had a presence, becoming a sort of template for an ADF response to this tragedy.

Ritual for Healing after Hurricane Katrina

Musical Signal

Honoring the Earth-Mother

> *O, Glorious womb of harvest.*
> *You fiery heart of creation.*
> *Gracious green mother.*
> *Earth Mother, accept this offering and uphold us in our rite.*
> (An offering of grain is made.)

All: Earth Mother, accept our offering.

Acknowledgement of the Outsiders

> *To You who stood against the gods.*
> *To You who stood against our forbearers.*
> *To You who stand against us.*
> *We thank you for the lessons you teach and the strength you build.*
> *Take this offering and trouble not our rite!*
> (A suitable offering is made outside the ritual area)

Specification of Ritual Purpose & Historical Precedent / Naming Deity of the Occasion

We gather together, joining with countless others across this continent, in order to remember those who have died as a result of Hurricane Katrina and to lend our prayers, our strength, and our energy to the continued effort to send relief and comfort to all those affected by this tragedy.

Centering, Grounding, & Merging
[Two Powers Meditation]

Offerings to the Sacred Center:
Acknowledgement of the Mundus

> *Sacred mundus, mouth of the Earth.*
> *Open for this brief time*
> *that we may receive all Numinae into our rite.*
> *Mundus patet!*

170

Acknowledgement of the Focus

Vesta Mater, Shining Lady, unite us all,
Queen of the hearth, Vesta Mater,
Your household is here.
Let us pray with a good fire.

Acknowledgement/Offering to the Focus

The folk stand as a doorway,
A pillar between the worlds.
Together, we gather at this sacred portal
In wisdom, love and hope.

Calling upon the Gate Keeper

Salve Ianus Pater!!
Ianus Inceptio, God of beginnings;
Ianus Brifons, Two-faced Ianus;
Ianus Patulcius, Opener of doors;
Ianus Domesticus, Protector of homes;
Ianus Quirinus; God of the folk
Lend wings to our prayers and conjure a portal between us and the
*   world of the Gods.*
Through your door, let the prayers of your supplicants pass to the
Kindreds.

Opening the Gates.

Janus, join your magic with mine
And let the focus open as a gate,
Let the mundus open as a gate,
Let the portus be the crossroads of all Worlds.

Ianus of Openings, admit us into the presence of the shining Ones
IANUS PATULCIUS ADMITTE NOS IN PRAESENTIUM NUMINUM
*   LUCENTIUM*
PORTAE APERIANTUR – Let the gates be open!

All: Let the Gates be open!

Offering to the Ancestors

The children of the Earth call out to the Mighty Dead.
Salvete, Majores et Di Manes!
Greetings, ancestors and divine dead.

You who have gone before,
Who fled in terror when Vesuvius erupted;
Who perished in floods, fires, wars and
Disasters, both natural and man-made.

Come to our hearth, Ancestors
Meet us at the boundary
Guide us and ward us as we walk the elder ways.

Majories et Di Manes, mactete hoc sacrificio!

All: Ancestors, accept our sacrifice!

Offering to the Nature Spirits

The children of the Earth call out to the Spirits of this Land.
Salvete, Numinae et Indigites!

Kindred of coastlands, wetlands and river valleys;
You whose homes and keepers have been lost or destroyed;
Who now wander, swim or crawl in confusion
In this world transformed from the familiar and safe.

Come to our fire, Spirits;
Meet us at the boundary.
Guide us and ward us as we walk the elder ways.

Numinae et Indigites, mactete hoc sacrificio!

All: Nature Spirits, accept our sacrifice!

Deities

The children of the Earth call out to the Shining Ones.
Salvete, Dei!

To all Gods and Goddesses:

172

You, who have held back the flood,
Who protect those who honor you when you can
And grieve by our sides when you cannot.

Come to our hearth, Shining Ones;
Meet us at the boundary.
Guide us and ward us as we walk the elder ways.

Dei, mactete hoc sacrificio!

All: Deities, accept our sacrifice!

The Main Sacrifice

Janus Pater, God of Beginnings, to those who have lost their homes and their communities:

> May You provide new beginnings, new homes, new jobs, and new friends to fill the empty places of those that were lost.

Hear our plea, Janus Pater.

All: Hear our plea, Janus Pater.

Tellus Mater, Mother Earth, to those whose loved ones have died and who are burdened by unimaginable losses, finding themselves refugees in their own country:

> May You provide comfort in the embrace of your loving arms.

Hear our plea, Tellus Mater.

All: Hear our plea, Tellus Mater.

Neptunus Pater, Provider of Fresh Water, to those areas inundated and polluted by flood water, debris and sewage:

> May You allow levees to be repaired, debris to be removed; help draw back the unclean waters and refresh those flooded areas with clean, pure water.

Hear our plea, Neptunus Pater.

All: Hear our plea, Neptunus Pater.

Fortuna Redux, Fortune, the Home-bringer, to those who fled their homes and inundated cities, who wonder if they will ever be able to return home or if they even have a home to return to:

> May You protect and steer them home when it is safe to return.

Hear our plea, Fortuna Redux.

All: Hear our plea, Fortuna Redux.

Aesculapius, God of Healing, to those who are injured, those separated and searching for family; to those who have been traumatized:
> May You be a healing presence in their lives for as long as it takes them to return to wholeness.

Hear our plea, Aesculapius.

All: Hear our plea, Aesculapius.

Spes, Goddess of Hope, to those who return to homes battered by wind and engulfed by flood and to those who have no homes to return to:
> May You provide hope that they may rebuild, reorganize, regroup and renew their homes and communities.

Hear our plea, Spes.

All: Hear our plea, Spes.

Mercurius, Protector of Travelers, to those who suffer on the streets or crowded into shelters, hot, weary, and fearful; to those who feel homesick and far away from loved ones and their homes at this time:
> May You provide the comfort of safe homes, rest and hospitality for as long as it is needed, comforting families and friends across the distance.

Hear our plea, Mercurius.

All: Hear our plea, Mercurius.

Ceres Mater, Provider of the Fruits of Earth, to those who have lost all material possessions; to the poor and those whose livelihoods have been lost or impaired by this disaster; to those whose workplaces have become unsafe and who face an uncertain future:
> May You provide sustenance and restore prosperity as quickly as possible.

Hear our plea, Ceres Mater.

All: Hear our plea, Ceres Mater.

Mars Olloudius, Protector of the People, to those who are involved in rescuing people and those caring for the injured in hospitals and clinics:
    May You sustain and uphold them through this time of tremendous loss and stress.

Hear our plea, Mars Olloudius.

All: Hear our plea, Mars Olloudius.

Quirinus, God of the Community, to those communities that have been devastated:
    May You help them live and learn and support one another and have joy in their lives once again; may this disaster bring people together to rebuild their cities, and to fill their lives with justice, their plates with food and their streets with music.

Hear our plea, Quirinus.

All: Hear our plea, Quirinus.

Jupiter Stator, to the police, firefighters, FEMA employees, National Guard, Red Cross workers, disaster response coordinators, whose work is just beginning and will not end for many months:
    May You strengthen and sustain them for service.

Hear our plea, Jupiter Stator.

All: Hear our plea, Jupiter Stator.

Vesta Mater, Embodiment of the Hearth Flame, to all those with home and without:
    May You warm their hearts, minds and bodies, bring them back to Your center.

Hear our plea, Vesta Mater.

All: Hear our plea, Vesta Mater.

Ancestors, Spirits and Gods, to each of us as we pray:
    May it be Your will to be propitious to us; may distance not deter us from generous giving and enduring companionship.

Hear our plea, Great Kindred.

All: Hear our plea, Great Kindred.

Piacular Offering

> *Gods and Goddesses,*
> *Holy Ancestors,*
> *Spirits of this place:*
> *If anything that we have done here has offended you,*
> *If anything we have done here has been incomplete,*
> *If anything we have done here has not been in the proper manner,*
> *Accept this final offering in recompense.*

Induction of Receptivity

> *Ancient and Mighty Ones, we have honored you*
> *and pray that you heed our prayers.*
> *For all those for whom we have petitioned,*
> *We ask that you hear your children:*

> *NUMINA LUCENTIA, AQUAE VIVAE DATIS!*
> All: Shining Ones, give us the Waters!

> *NUMINA LUCENTIA, AQUAE VIVAE DATIS!*
> All: Shining Ones, give us the Waters!

> *NUMINA LUCENTIA, AQUAE VIVAE DATIS!*
> All: Shining Ones, give us the Waters!

Consecration Agreement

> *Behold the holy Cup of Magic*
> *The outpouring of Blessing from the Great Ones*
> *When we share the draught of the Gods*
> *We drink in wisdom, love and strength*
> *To do as we will in the worlds*
> *In service to the Shining Ones.*

> *Hear us Mighty Kindred:*
> *Hallow these waters with your blessings!*

> *ECCE AQUAE VIVAE!*

All: Behold the Waters of Life!

(The cup is shared.)

Thanking of Entities Invited in Reverse Order

The Great Ones have blessed us.
Let us carry the magic from our sacred Grove
Into our lives and our work.

Each time we offer to the Powers
They become stronger
And more aware of our needs and our worship.

So now as we prepare to depart
Let us give thanks
To all those who have aided us.

Janus Pater, Tellus Mater, Neptunus Pater, Fortuna Redux, Aesculapius, Spes, Mercurius, Ceres Mater, Mars Olloudius, Quirinus, Jupiter Stator, and Vesta Mater, we thank you.

All: We thank you!

Gods and Goddesses of elder days, we thank you.
All: We thank you!

O Spirits of this land , we thank you.
All: We thank you!

O Ancestors, our Kindred, we thank you.
All: We thank you!

To all those Powers that have aided us, we thank you.
All: We thank you!

Mother of all
To you we return all we leave unused
Uphold us now in the world as you have in our rite.
Earth Mother, we thank you.
All: We thank you!

Ianus Clusivius, closer of doors,
For your presence and power
Your guiding and guarding we thank you.
All: We thank you!

Affirmation of Past/Future Continuity and Success

> *Now by the Keeper of Gates and by our magic*
> *We end what we began.*
>
> *Now let the Focus be but a flame;*
> *Let the Mundus be but a pot;*
> *Let the Portus be only a doorway.*
> *Let all be as it was before...*
>
> *PORTAE CLAUDANTUR!!*

All: Let the Gates be closed!

> *Go now, Quirites*
> *In peace and blessings*
> *The rite is ended!*

Samonios

By Rev. Michael J Dangler

This ritual works very strongly in my own personal pantheon, but it's easily adapted for whatever you wish to do. It's called Samonios, rather than Samhain, because it's a Gaulish-focused ritual. It also runs very strictly off the ADF Core Order of Ritual.

1. Enter Space

2. Prepare Space

- Light candles
- Fill well

3. Opening Prayers

Earth Mother

I stand firm on you, Earth Mother
You are a keeper of vision,
The one in whom the portal is rooted
The one who offers me passage
The one to whom I must always return.
Earth Mother, you support me
Support and uphold my rite.

Inspiration

I reach deeply within myself;
  seeking, searching.
My eyes turn inward and see deep;
  seeking, searching.
My fingers reach out, feeling forth;
  seeking, searching.
My ears are open, listening;
  seeking, searching.
My nose sniffs for any sign here;
  seeking, searching.
My tongue tastes the sweet nectar now;
  seeking, searching.
Here it is, within me, calling;
  seeking, searching.
Here I am, to greet it, hold it;
  seeking, searching.
Here we are, together, tightly;
  holding, knowing.
Inspiration, I call to you;
  hold me, know me.

4. Purpose

Say something pretty in celebration of Samonios, honoring Cernunnos, honoring the Dead.

5. Purification

- Outdwellers → no need
- Space → taken care of before
- Self → taken care of before, but include a "reminding" of purification

6. Gatekeeper

Garanus

One foot in the water, Crane
One foot on land.
One eye in the blue sky, Crane
Always between.
The realms are your plaything
Ever your joy
Guide me through them this day

Old Ways I walk.
No one knows better, Crane
The ways between the worlds.

Opening the Gates

Garanus Crane
Open the gates
    Fire comes first
    Well is second
    The Tree is third
Open the Gates
Garanus Crane
Open the Gates.

7. Calling to All: Chthonics/Mids/Uppers[9]

Calling to the Upper Kindreds

High in the Heavens, Heroes and Holy
Beyond the visible reaches of the Sky
Beyond the Veil of the Stars and Sun
Those Kindred that shine with light from Above
Shining Ones, Ancestors, Nature Spirits
Far-Seeing and Brightly clothed in gold light
Come to my Fire, offerings for Thee
A welcome to the Powers of Heaven
Be comfortable in my abode tonight.

Calling to the Middle Kindreds

Here among us are Gods and Dead and Sidhe
Standing within mists, coming to meet us
Coming nearer as we give offering
Standing next to us in our times of need.
In trees and streams, under foot, in the air
The Spirits of Place surround us always
Their songs reach our ears, their beauty our eyes
I call welcome to Spirits of this Realm
Be comfortable in my abode tonight.

---

[9] I decided on a different kind of "Three Kindred" invocation because of the High Day involved. Rather than doing "NS, Ancestors, Deities," I chose to do "Kindreds of the Heavens/Middleworld/Underworld," and each invocation deals with the 3 Kindred as you can find them in each realm. As I look back on it, I like it even more.

Calling to the Chthonic Kindreds

Down below our feet, deep within the ground
In the fertile womb of the Earth Mother
Are denizens of Dark, unknown to us:
Gods of the Earth, Ancestors, and Earth-Kin.
Our bones will rest here though our soul will rise
Now we pour libation to these Kindred
Knowing their place in life and the Cosmos
I welcome the spirits of Dark Earth.
Be comfortable in my abode tonight.

8. Key Offerings

Cernunnos, Antlered God,
I call out to you now.
You sit in doorways,
seeing both directions

Open the Veil you hold,
part it like warm butter.[10]
Allow the Ancestors
to come forth this dark night.

Cernunnos, Between Ways,
Accept this offering!

[Praise should now be offered to Cernunnos, and to the Ancestors.]

9. Prayer of Sacrifice

Cernunnos, Guardian,
You who have spread the veil,
You who have brought our ancestors,
I ask that you return them,
That you close the veil.
Whisper to them that they are not forgotten,
And allow them to leave any blessings they may.
Cernunnos, Accept this sacrifice!

10. Omen

Take as usual.

---

[10] I think I was thinking about Agni, what with the "butter" and stuff. But it works for me.

11. Calling the Blessings

Cernunnos, Shining Ones!
We have given and you have answered us in kind!
I call now for the blessings you offer
Pour them out to us,
Offer them now!

12. Hallowing

Within this cup, the outpouring of your love
Within this cup, the reciprocal flow of return
Consecrate these waters with your power, Shining Ones
That I may drink deeply from them.

13. Affirmation

Indeed the cup is blessed,
and by drinking deeply,
I am blessed in turn.
It wells within me, mingling,
and completes me.

14. Workings

None.

15. Thanking

In reverse order: Cernunnos, Lower/Mid/Upper Kindreds, Other Powers, Gatekeeper

16. Closing the Gates

Garanus Crane
Close the gates
    The Tree comes first
    The Well second
    Fire is third
Close the Gates
Garanus Crane
Close the Gates.

17. Thanking the Earth Mother

Earth Mother, to you I will return all I have left unused.
Uphold me now in life as you have in this rite.
I thank you!

18. Closing the Rite
This rite is ended!

Yule Rite

By Rev. Michael J Dangler

[If you're using this rite yourself, make sure you've read through it and have necessary sacrifices you wish to make. Note that I didn't include any specific sacrifices or offerings, because I think it's best if you choose how much or how little to offer. This entire rite can be done without a single offering, but, as Ceisiwr Serith says, "When we come before the gods, it is wise not to come empty-handed." You will need a few things for the rite: a representation of a tree, three votive candles (in holders), a vessel of water of some kind, something to drink from, and some way to take an omen. Anything else is window-dressing. The Patron of this rite is Sulis, a Gaulish sun goddess, so don't be surprised if you find feminine pronouns for the sun. Many prayers (Gatekeeper invocation, song for the return of the sun, and the opening of the Gates, for example) are straight from Ceisiwr Serith's <u>A Book of Pagan Prayer</u>.*]*

The Yule Rite:

Enter Sacred Space, stand before the altar.

State purpose: "Hail the Sun! Today I welcome you back from the darkness!"

Fill the well, Light one of the three candles.

Mother Earth invocation:
(place hands on the floor/ground)

I call out to the Earth Mother
You who support me.
You who hold me
You who has birthed me and will once again take me.
Earth Mother, in her daily travels, the sun passes through you.
Her path has grown longer with each passing day
Since the last Solstice, this summer gone.
It is in your power to shorten this trail
The lonely one through your tunnels and caves
I ask that you hear your children
And show her the way.

Inspiration:

(face the fire)

Snow and ice have cooled our minds
Cold winds have blown away our fertile thoughts
Silent nights have stilled our tongues
Like the bear, the fox, and the toad
Our creativity hibernates without the warmth of the sun.
Come to us now, Inspiration, as the sun returns!
As the sun grows in strength
So may the fire in our hearts!

Purpose restatement:

(face altar)

"Today, the sun is renewed. The long descent into darkness is ended, the long night is halfway over. I look forward at this time, remembering what I have done, knowing what I will do. I make promises to myself and to the Gods. Most of all, though, I welcome in Sulis, the sun herself, and pray that the increase of her light also show an increase in my blessings. Hail the Sun!"

Outdwellers:

(face north and hold up your hands)

From far to the North do these things come:
Cold North Wind, biting and raw.
Ice Storms, piercing and painful
Sleet, Snow, and Slush, dangerous and underestimated
Alberta Clipper, snowy and feared.
Lake Effect Snow, plentiful and inconvenient
In-Laws, We're not home!
I name these things at this time, the things I wish to see less of in this season, and I set them aside.

Attunement: 2 Powers meditation. You can do the standard one, or you can be a bit creative. As an example, I'm thinking of the Two Powers we all thought about around this time of year: the Naughty and Nice powers.

Sacred Center: dip your finger in the well, pass your hand over the flame, and touch the tree. Feel the connection to each of the gates.

Gatekeeper invocation:

(face the well)

Cernunnos, lord, sitter in the doorway
God of equilibrium, terrible, merciful:
You who hold the opposites apart,
You in whom all opposites unite,
My prayer goes to you to open the passage
To clear the threshold,
To make the way clear.

Opening the Gates:

Open the way
Open the way
Lord Cernunnos
Open the way

(make an opening triskel over the Well; envision it as a gate to the Underworld)

Open the way
Open the way
Lord Cernunnos
Open the way

(make an opening triskel over the Fire; envision it as a gate to the Upperworld)

Open the way
Open the way
Lord Cernunnos
Open the way

(make an opening triskel over the tree; envision it as the crossroads of the Worlds)

Let the Gates be Opened!

Ancestors invocation:

(face the well)

I call out to those who came before me
Hear me, O ancestors!
The sun has traveled through your lands
In an ever-lengthening journey.

I ask that you remember the cold winters of your lives
Remember the piercing winds
Remember the ice and the darkness.
Remember that your descendants feel this now.
I call out to you, and ask that you join me.
Together, let us encourage the sun to return,
For she has traveled in your world long,
And now it is time for her to travel in mine.
Welcome, and thanks to the Ancestors!

Nature Spirits invocation:

(face the tree or open window)

A child of the earth calls out to the spirits of this place
Hear me, spirits of nature!
Though it is cold outside
And many of you sleep beneath the ground
Or in nests high above my head,
I ask that you hear my voice,
And join your call to mine
As I call the sun back to the skies
To bring her warmth and shining love
For all of us to feel.
Welcome, and thanks to the Nature Spirits!

Deities invocation:

(face the fire)

Your child calls out to you, Elder Gods.
Hear me, O deities!
The sun has fulfilled her old bargain,
She has taken the long roads through the Underworld.
She has distanced herself from the lands of the living.
She has allowed the cold, the snow, and the ice
To gather about us, as you have declared she should.
Now is the time that we may ask for her return.
Tonight, we call out to your sense of justice,
Your sense of love for us,
And ask that you join with us in calling her back.
Welcome, and thanks to the Deities!

186

Welcoming of the Kindred:

(place hands palms up before your body, smile, and shout)

Welcome to my Ancestors, the Nature Spirits, and the Gods!
Now, I ask that you join me in my call to the Patroness of this rite!

Calling in the Sun:

(facing the fire, and especially the two unlit candles)

Sulis, Sun Maiden,
Bright wheel in the sky!
Hear me as I call out to you
And pray for your safe return
And increase this solstice day!

Six months ago, I reveled in your height
I sang in the fields as you rose,
Strong and proud and full of splendor.
Since then, I have watched you lessen
Until the equinox, when you gave summer to the Underworld.

Your path has been long and dark
But you have lit the way for souls
Who have long departed this world.
You spent time under the earth
Moving through tunnels and caverns
Each day longer ones than before
And my ancestors appreciate the light.

But now it is time for you to return.
You have not forgotten those still living
Who now need your light more than ever
For our nights have become too long,
Too cold, too quiet.
It is right that you should return to us.

So, O Sulis, Lady of the Sun,
I ask you that you return to us,
Bringing with you the warmth
We so desperately need.
Find shorter passages through the Underworld;
Take the fastest route back to us.

Do not leave us to freeze in this cold winter.

Sulis, with this candle lit, [light first candle]
Find your way through the dark of the Underworld.
Sulis, with this candle lit, [light second candle]
Find your strength, and remember the old bargains.

Sulis, the light of the world has returned!

Final sacrifices:

(if not making offerings, cut text appropriately)

I have made offerings to Sulis
The Deities, the Nature Spirits, and my Ancestors.
Now, Sulis, I pray you accept my offerings
And that you bring the sun back for another bright year.

Omen:

(Take omen as you usually would. If all omens point to a positive outcome, use the
following prayer of praise:)

On the rim of the world, She is dancing.
In Her bright robe, She is dancing.
Young and lovely, She is dancing.
Bringer of vision, She is dancing.
Dance, Sun Maiden, into the sky,
Bringing the day to those who wait for you.

Return Flow:

(elevate drink of water/wine/mead/etc., and speak)

I draw blessing from the cauldron of blessing
I pour the mead of inspiration
Behold, the holy cup of magic!
Into it flows the outpouring of all blessings
The deities would grant me,
And when I partake of the drink of the gods,
I am accepting the power to do as I will in the worlds.
(drink)

Thanks and closing:

Now, I close this rite.
But first, let me thank those who have offered help:
Sulis, for your power, protection, and returning light,
I thank you.
Deities, for your upholding the bargains,
I thank you.
Nature Spirits, for adding your voice to mine,
I thank you.
Ancestors, for giving up the sun and allowing the descent into winter,
I thank you.
Earth Mother, for showing the sun the proper ways,
I thank you.
To all the powers who have here aided me,
I say again, I thank you.
Finally, O Gatekeeper, I thank you, but I ask one final boon.

Closing the Gates:

Close the way
Close the way
Lord Cernunnos
Close the way

    (make a Closing triskel over the Well; envision it as a gate to the Underworld)

Close the way
Close the way
Lord Cernunnos
Close the way

    (make a Closing triskel over the Fire; envision it as a gate to the Upperworld)

Close the way
Close the way
Lord Cernunnos
Close the way

    (make a Closing triskel over the tree; envision it as the crossroads of the Worlds)

Let the Gates be Closed!

Ending the rite

(empty all unused offerings to the earth, or into a bowl for later disposal)

I return all I leave unused to the Earth.
This rite is ended!
The Sun has returned!

Family-Oriented Ostara

By Anna Gail

I performed this ritual Ostara of 2007 with two of my children and three more children that belonged to a friend of mine. There was only one other adult present so I had to make this quick and simple for the kids. Not an easy task. The whole ritual only took 40 minutes.

Statement of Purpose: The welcoming of spring to the land.

Processional: Walked to the altar singing 'We Approach the Sacred Grove' - Words by Sean Miller

> *We approach the sacred grove,*
> *With hearts and minds and flesh and bone,*
> *Join us now in ways of old,*
> *We have come home.*

Now this particular part usually sounds like a dirge, however by speeding the tempo up and singing it in a slightly higher key, the kids made is sound a lot more upbeat and sacred. We also included a tambourine and a small drum to keep the tempo light.

Offerings to the outsiders: A whole gallon of mead that I had made was offered to a corner of the yard that was a bit shady and kind of eerie looking due to excess foliage.

Hammer Rite: This is a basic blessing where you make the sign of the hammer (Thor's) in each of the four directions then above and below saying the following:

> *Hammer of the (direction), hold and hallow this holy stead*

My oldest son really enjoyed this part. He had to be shown which direction to turn, but his voice carried quite nicely.

Honoring the Earth Mother ~ Nerthus

Nerthus was an ancient Germanic earth goddess. Tacitus recorded that each year there was a festival where the goddess would supposedly travel in a chariot pulled by two white heifers, escorted by the priest. No one was allowed to take up war or bear arms during the festivities. Even iron tools were locked up during the goddess' journey. It was good luck for those settlements she visited in her journey.

At this point we sang another song. The kids really liked to sing, and they thought this song was very pretty and simple:

Blossom Lifter
[Traditional Romova, via JD Labash and StoneCreed Grove, ADF]

Earth Mother, Blossom Lifter
Bless what we eat,
Bless what we drink,
Bless what we harrow,
And bless what we sow.
Earth Mother, Blossom Lifter
Bloom with the wheat
Bloom with the rye
Bloom with barley,
And Bloom with all grain
Earth Mother, Blossom Lifter
With all these things,
Let us rejoice...
You give to us,
And we give to you.

Offerings were then made to the Earth Mother (my daughter offered cornmeal)

Bardic Inspiration ~ Bragi
My son did this part as well. He mainly said, 'please don't let us say something bad'. Simple and to the point. I liked it.

Grounding and Meditation (desperately needed at this point due to the children, but was accomplished by simply having the kids close their eyes and take a couple of deep breaths)

Gatekeeper ~ Norns (I offered incense as we were outside)

Opening the gates ~ lighting the candles to the 9 realms
    Asgard – land of the Aesir
    Vanaheim – land of the Vanir
    Alfheim – land of the Alfar

Midgard – land of man
Jotenheim – land of the frost giants
Muspelheim – land of fire
Helheim – land of the dead/ancestors
Niflheim – land of ice
Svartalfheim – land of dwarves

All this entailed was having the kids take turns lighting the candles and opening the gates. They did so by saying

'With this candle burning bright, let the gates of (name) be opened wide.'

It was short and simple. And by making it sort of rhyme the kids were able to remember for each gate. The tricky part was teaching them how to pronounce the various realms.

Once all the candles were lit, we all threw our arms out and shouted 'Let the gates be open!'

Offerings to the three Kindreds were made while singing the portal song - Words and music by Ian Corrigan © Stonecreed Grove, ADF:

<u>Chorus:</u>
By Fire and by Water, between the Earth and Sky
We stand like the World-Tree rooted deep, crowned high.

Come we now to the Well, the eye and the mouth of Earth,
Come we now to the Well, and silver we bring,
Come we now to the Well, the waters of rebirth,
Come we now to the Well, together we sing
Chorus
We will kindle a fire, Bless all, and with harm to none,
We will kindle a Fire, and offering pour,
We will kindle a Fire, A light 'neath the Moon & Sun,
We will kindle a fire, our spirits will soar
Chorus
Gather we at the Tree, the root & the crown of all,
Gather we at the Tree, Below & above,
Gather we at the Tree, Together we make our call,
Gather we at the Tree, In wisdom and love.
Chorus

Coming from another group, we sang the chorus twice in between each verse. We also clapped our hands, tapped our feet, swayed, danced and sang louder and with

192

smiles on our faces. I have taught my children that honoring the Kindreds should be a joyful, happy experience. This song is NOT a slow one, nor is it a dirge. By making it fun and bouncy the kids learned it faster and loved to participate.

Deity of the Occasion: Eostre

We had made colored, hardboiled eggs for decorating her altar. We also had a plate of goodies that we offered. Eggs, fruit, and the first flowers of spring were all decorating the hearth and placed on a plate specifically for Eostre. Remember, with kids you have to keep it on their level.

Omen ~ Runes

For this I had each of the children draw a rune (three total) and gave them the basic meaning for each rune. I then had them 'meditate' on how they thought that rune applied to the group as a whole. While I do not remember what the actual reading was, I do remember that what they came up with was actually very good. Having the kids participate and actively work within the ritual made them want to do more.

Sumble ~ passing the horn one time around the group accepting the blessings of the reading and honoring any other deities they felt called to.

Thanked and said goodbye to Eostre

Thanked the Kindreds

Closed the gates – put out the candles while saying:

Now the candle light is gone, let the gates of (name) be closed

(this didn't rhyme but it was still simple) Once all the candles were out, we then closed our arms around ourselves and shouted 'Let the gates be closed'

Children are very visual and physical. By having us throw our arms out to open the gates and then close them around ourselves at the end it helped the children know that there was a definite difference and gave them a clue that things were winding   down.

Thanked the Norns for watching the gates

Thanked Bragi (as my son would say 'For not letting us say anything bad')

Thanked the Earth Mother

"This rite is ended."

We then feasted in the house to celebrate spring.

Chants and Songs

This Grove has also written some excellent chants through the years. Here are some that we have heard as invocations, praise offerings, and throughout our worship.

Drumming 9 Fold Prayer
By Shawneen

thrum... thrum... thrum...
Land and Sky And Sea
Fire and Well and Tree
Totems And Mothers And Goddesses on high
Come to us now and be with us nigh
Thrum...thrum....thrum...
Land and Sky And Sea
Fire and Well and Tree
Totems And Fathers And Gods up on high
Come to us now and be with us nigh
Thrum...thrum....thrum...

Shawneen also says of the above: "I have been using a few stanzas of it as my two powers meditation/trance induction in my own personal devotions. I find drawing out the last word of each line creates a nice sonorous song line. Give it a try! Enjoy!" It is to be chanted while drumming (the "thrums" are continuous beats on the drum).

Brighid Chant
By Anna Banana

We are singing here to honor bright and shining Brighid.
You who forge in fires brilliant lands of fertile green.

Kindle hope and thought inspire,
Dancing like the flame.
Light our hearts with sacred fire,
Dancing like the flame.

You of healing, smithing, feeling, bright protectress Brighid:
Guide us now with strength and purpose, root us like the trees.

Kindreds Song

By Seamus

(Chorus)
Standing at the sacred center
Standing at the sacred Tree
Offerings to Kindreds
For the blessing they've given me
Oil for the sacred Fire
Silver for the holy Well
Offerings to the Kindreds
For the blessings I hope to see

(Verse one)
Praise to the dearly departed
Praise to the mighty dead
Hail to the Ancestors
Of our heart, our spirit, our head

(Repeat Chorus)

(Verse two)
Praise to the Noble Ones,
Praise to the mighty Sidhe
Hail to the spirits of nature,
The earth, the sky, and the sea

(Verse three)
Praise to our Mother's first Children
Praise to the bright Deities
Hail to the wise and mighty ones
Let your blessing shine down on me.

(Repeat Chorus)

Shawneen's sylvan muses have gifted him with the following chant: (Previously published in Crane Chatter, our newsletter.)

Transpiration/Inspiration

By Shawneen

Take it up
Let it go
Within us now
Begin to flow
Call it down
We knit the round
Within us know
We need to grow

Mannanan Chant

By Anna Banana

Mannanan, a grey mist falling
Mannanan, on rolling waves
Mannanan, the seabirds calling
Mannanan, oe'r an old whale's grave

Mannanan, Mannanan-Mannanan,
Mannanan, Man-na-nan
(repeat)

Mannanan, a faint path clearing
Mannanan, through glassy seas
Mannanan, the helmsman steers us
Mannanan, for the dawn he has seen

Mannanan, Mannanan-Mannanan,
Mannanan, Man-na-nan
(repeat)

Healing Chant

By Shawneen

Prayers are whispered
Chants are sung
The Kindred are listening
The healing's begun!

Cernunnos Chant

By Anna Banana

Cernunnos, answer our call
Your children honor your name
Though autumns fade and summers may die
Your fire within us remains

Cernunnos, answer our call
Your children honor your name
You hold the light and darkness apart
We dance with both in our hearts

Open the Gates (Cernunnos Chant)

By Anna Banana

Close, the howling of the wolves
Yet far our song must carry
Through the doorways of the dead
Where ancient kin lay buried

Cernunnos
Cernunnos
Cernunnos
Open the gates

Bright the circle of the flame
Yet dark the shadowed forest
Raise our voices not in vain
But bright and fearless chorus

Cernunnos
Cernunnos
Cernunnos
Open the gates

Thanking Song

By Rev. Michael J Dangler

For all who have gathered
And all who have come,
We thank you for presence
And all you have done.

For blessings you've given
And joining us here,
You Shining Ones hold us
And we hold you dear.

For letting us dwell here
And joining our rite,
You spirits of nature
We thank you this night.

For going before us
And showing the way,
Ancestors of our folk
Your honor we pay.

For offerings given
And blessings received,
We stand forth in Ghosti,
Re-ci-pro-ci-ty.

Once when he was young (too young to write chants, for sure), our Grove Priest posted a chant to an ADF email list, offering it as a processional in the great tradition of ADF chants: dirge-like and kind of silly. While the joke was not seen as humorous by all, it did help bring a bit of creativity back to ADF's chants. Since this chant was posted, ADF's Bards have written some amazing chants that put this one to shame.

Are We There Yet? (Processional)

By Rev. Michael J Dangler

[the "folk" part should be sung as slowly and monotonously as possible. The "leader" part should be sung as exasperatedly as possible]

Folk: Are we there yet?

Leader: NO!
Folk: Are we there yet?
Leader: NO!
Folk: Are we there yet?
Leader: NO!
Folk: Are we there yet?
Leader: (upon arrival to the sacred space) YES!

Other variations on the above chant have grown up in ADF, with the most noticeable one being a changing response by the Leader, which might go like this:

Leader: Let us approach the Sacred Grove. Please be patient: it's a long way. You'd better have all gone to the bathroom as I asked. (begins drumming and walking)
Folk: Are we there yet?
Leader: NO!
Folk: Are we there yet?
Leader: I told you, NO!
Folk: Are we there yet?
Leader: Stop asking that!
Folk: Are we there yet?
Leader: Don't make me turn this procession around!
Folk: Are we there yet?
Leader: (upon arrival to the sacred space) YES!

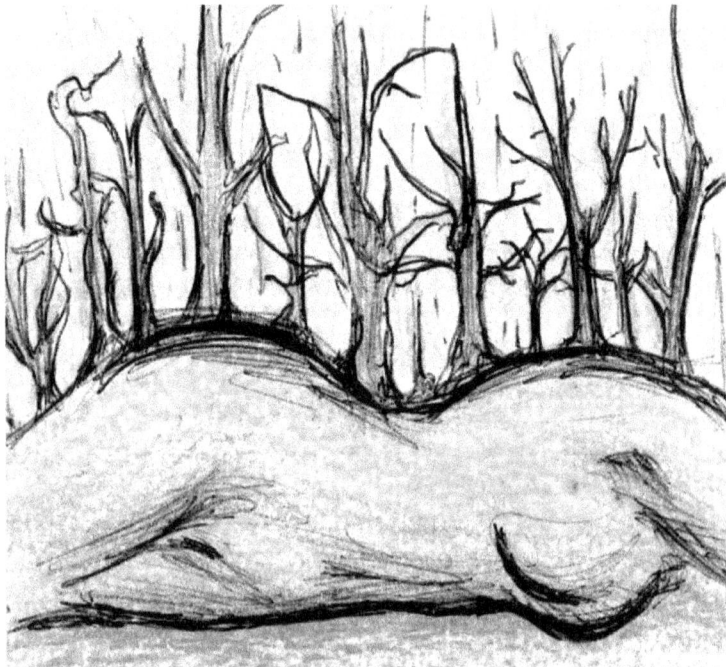

A Kindred Prayer

Bess Closs/Melissa Burchfield

Voice 1 (line 1):
To a log we set fire for the new year to come, wi-th
As we walk with the old ones, the youg and the new, we re-
The__ child-ren cheer, laugh-ing, color'd ribbons deck a pole, Wi-ld

Voice 1 (line 2):
ma - ny mead pours as a bles-sing for some. Drum beats sur - round us as
tell all their stor - ies with morn-ing's first dew. Sha-dows hide se - crets that
Spir-its come play, lured from their win - ter holes. The trees do they whis-per

A Kindred Prayer

flames dance with wind; in - vi - ted are those from the ma - ny Hearth kins.
heal our dear Earth, our les-sons we've learned from their tears and their mirth.
flow - ers they sing The wa-ters they tend and the life that it brings.

Pno.

O, Shi - ning Ones._____ We of - fer a prayer!_____
O, An - cest - ors._____ We of - fer a prayer!_____
O, No - ble Ones._____ We of - fer a prayer!_____

Pno.

A Kindred Prayer

Shi - ning Ones be - side me you stay. day af - ter day ne'er turn-ing a-
Might - y Dead, in my heart you'll re - main un - til one day, we me - et a-
Bro - thers and Sis - ters of the land, with-in your footsteps you le - et me

Pno.

way. _____ Kin - dred three, you care for me: Kin - dred Three, I
gain. _____
stand. _____

Pno.

A Kindred Prayer

hon - or Thee. Kin - dred Three, you care for me; Kin - dred Three, I

Kin - dred Three, you care for me; Kin - dred Three, I

Pno.

hon - or Thee. Kin - dred Three, you care for me; Kin - dred Three, I

hon - or Thee. Kin - dred Three, you care for me; Kin - dred Three, I

Pno.

A Kindred Prayer

honor Thee. Kindred Three, you care for me;
honor Thee. Shining Ones, in my heart you'll remain, day after

Kindred Three I honor Thee. Kindred Three, you
day, ne'er turning away. Mighty Dead, in my heart you'll re-

A Kindred Prayer

care for me; Kin-dredThree, I hon-or Thee. Kin - dred Three, you

main, un - til one day, when we meet a - gain._____ Bro thers and sis ters of the

Pno.

care for me; Kin - dred Three, I hon - or Thee. O,

land, with - in your footsteps you let me stand._____ O,

Pno.

A Kindred Prayer

Teutates

Melissa S. Burchfield

Care fu - ly, the gar - den - er tends the trees._____ One by one, in -
Sca - tered seeds, he gath-ered us in his hand._____ Root-ed deep, the

spect - ing all the leaves_____ Re - mov-ing all the parts_____ out grown, En-
seed-lings now strong-ly stand. With love and care through all_____ the years, In

cour - ag - ing new life_____ to grow, Let-ting all the green_____ parts see the light_____
good and ill he per - se-veres, to see us grow 'til_____ we are all crwoned

high Teu - ta - tes, Gen - tle God_____ of all the tribe_____
Teu - ta - tes, stead - fast tend - er of the tribe._____

Known to each in his_____ or her own way._____ Heal - ing us Pro-tect -

- ing us, Be - side us day to day._____ He guides us on the El - der path, He

makes our fu tures bright. Teu - ta - tes Might-y Keep - er of the tribe!_____ Teu

ta - tes con - se-crate_____ our hum ble Grove_____ il - lu-min-ate us stir our ver - y souls__

Teutates

In - sp - ire us with strength____ and fire, In fuse us to our hearts____

de-sire Drench us and su-fuse____ us with your rains,____ Teu-

ta - tes, Might-y Pa - tron of the Cranes.____ Known to each in his__

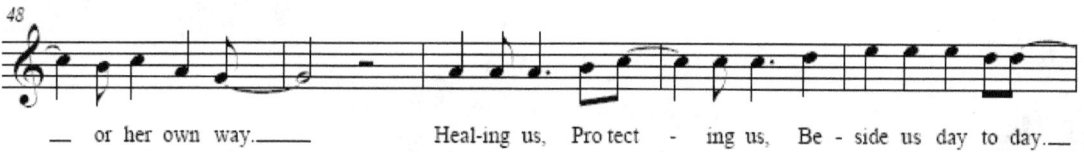

__ or her own way.____ Heal-ing us, Pro tect - ing us, Be - side us day to day.__

__ He guides us on the El - der path, He makes our fu tures bright. Teu

ta - tes Might - y Keep - er of the tribe!____ Teu - ta - tes in your arms__

__ we sa - tis-fi____ ed.____ Teu - ta - tes Un - i-fi - er of__ the tribe!

Further Reading

There are a number of books, resources, and websites that are strongly recommended for further reading and study, and we hope that our members will always go back to these resources whenever they begin to work through ritual.

Ceisiwr Serith: A Book of Pagan Prayer

This is the book that has most strongly influenced the Grove's voice, and every member of the Grove should own a copy. Cei is an ADF member, and has been the source of much of ADF's ritual language and central cosmology. As a result, he can be considered foundational to the Grove's own voice (despite, as of this writing, never attending a Grove rite), as his voice was filtered through our first Grove Priest, Rev. Jenni Hunt, and affected our first rituals through her.

The Rgveda (Walter H. Maurer translation)

The Rgveda is the oldest complete set of hymns and praises to Indo-European gods, and possibly the oldest complete holy book in existence. The praises and prayers contained within the Rgveda, and one of our most oft-quoted statements about our piety and action comes directly from the RV: "Let us pray with a good fire." (RV I.26.8)

A.A. MacDonnell: Vedic Mythology

This book outlines and cross-references all the deities and the cosmology of the Vedics, and has served as an invaluable reference for prayers and ritual ideas through the years.

ADF Standard Liturgical Outline, 6th Night's outline, and 3CG ritual scripts

Of course, the ADF Standard Liturgy is the grandmother of our own rituals, but The 6th Night Grove, ADF, wrote a standard liturgy that Three Cranes used for the first few rites, and our ritual has developed along its own lines from there. Our rituals have been adapted recently to refocus on the ADF Core Order of Ritual when it comes to High Day rites, but since the COoR only regards High Day rites, the Grove still plays around a lot with the ordering of our rituals, keeping them organic and alive with change.

Oak Leaves, the ADF Website, Festivals, and Grove events

The most important places to find what's new and organic are the publications and gatherings of ADF members. If you can get a subscription to OL, get one. If you can get to a festival, go. You'll be surprised at the good material you can find there!

GARANUS PUBLISHING

www.ingramcontent.com/pod-product-compliance
Lightning Source LLC
Chambersburg PA
CBHW062040090426
42740CB00016B/2972